Sonia Moore and American Acting Training

With a Sliver of Wood in Hand

Suzanne M. Trauth
Elizabeth C. Stroppel

THE SCARECROW PRESS, INC.
Lanham, Maryland • *Toronto* • *Oxford*
2005

SCARECROW PRESS, INC.

Published in the United States of America
by Scarecrow Press, Inc.
A wholly owned subsidiary of
The Rowman & Littlefield Publishing Group, Inc.
4501 Forbes Boulevard, Suite 200, Lanham, Maryland 20706
www.scarecrowpress.com

PO Box 317
Oxford
OX2 9RU, UK

British Library Cataloguing in Publication Information Available

Library of Congress Cataloging-in-Publication Data
Trauth, Suzanne.
  Sonia Moore and American acting training : with a sliver of wood in hand /
Suzanne M. Trauth, Elizabeth C. Stroppel.
    p. cm.
  Includes bibliographical references and index.
  ISBN 0-8108-5678-6 (pbk. : alk. paper)
  1. Moore, Sonia. 2. Acting teachers—United States—Biography. 3. Method
(Acting) I. Stroppel, Elizabeth C. II. Title.
  PN2287.M6974T73 2005
  792.02'8'071—dc22
                                                                2005007747

⊗™ The paper used in this publication meets the minimum requirements of
American National Standard for Information Sciences—Permanence of Paper
for Printed Library Materials, ANSI/NISO Z39.48-1992.

Manufactured in the United States of America

Contents

Acknowledgments

Books rarely make it to the shelves without the efforts of many people. Countless words are read, listened to, analyzed, organized, contextualized, written, and rewritten to produce a final draft. This book is no exception. To the following people and institutions we offer our sincerest gratitude:

Irene Moore, who generously provided us with her mother's memoirs and photograph, as well as recollections of Sonia Moore in both a personal and professional capacity.

Philip G. Bennett, Linda S. Chapman, Elizabeth D'Onofrio, Vincent D'Onofrio, Frone Lund, Jane Marla Robbins, and Len Silver, for sharing their reminiscences of training, performing, and teaching at the Sonia Moore Studio of the Theatre, in addition to their stories about Sonia Moore.

Sharon M. Carnicke of the University of Southern California, for her advice and invaluable text, and Robert Barton of the University of Oregon and David Krasner of Yale University, for reading our manuscript and providing us with enormously insightful comments about it.

Montclair State University and William Paterson University, for supporting this endeavor by granting us release time to research and write *Sonia Moore and American Acting Training: With a Sliver of Wood in Hand*. We also thank the students of these institutions, as well as those of the Sonia Moore Studio, who allowed us the privilege of exploring Sonia Moore's work with them. Without their enthusiasm, curiosity, and willingness to experiment, we would have been unable to complete this project.

The staff at the New York Public Library for the Performing Arts, and Sara Weissman in the Reference Department of the Morris County Library.

Stephen Ryan at Scarecrow Press, for recognizing the potential of this book and for always being close to his e-mail to answer our questions.

Each of us has personal debts as well:

Thanks to Patricia Relph, whose request that I replace her at a theatre convention resulted in my meeting Sonia Moore in the summer of 1986. I appreciate Phil Cuomo's friendship during our last years at the Studio and his gracious offer to read early drafts of this book. Thanks also to Mary McTigue for her helpful feedback.

I am extremely grateful for the moral support of my mother, Martha, and my sisters—Denise, Eileen, Jeanette, Patty, Kate, and especially Charlene, who was there from the beginning. Over the years they cheered me on, listening patiently. Thanks also to Ron Harvey and Kathy Driehaus for lending their technical expertise. I would particularly like to thank Liz for joining me in this adventure without knowing where we might end up. I appreciate her meticulous research, editing wisdom, generosity of spirit, and willingness to go the extra mile when it most counted.

Finally, my love and thanks to Elaine Insinnia for her belief in me and in this project, for reading various versions of the book, and for always encouraging my work in the theatre, wherever it has taken me.

—Suzanne Trauth

To the Stroppel family, my friends, colleagues, and faith, I offer more thanks than the publisher will allow me to print. To Sue, I extend my sincerest appreciation for the opportunity to write this book about a woman whom we both admired so similarly yet differently and about whom each of us has such passionate memories. Her planning, energy, determination, critical analysis, and friendship have made this process a special one, including those twelve-hour rewriting sessions, chocolate-chip cookies in hand!

—Elizabeth Stroppel

Finally, we are thankful to Sonia Moore. Without her, there would be no book. As we wrote and revised this manuscript, we sometimes believed that she was looking down on us, prodding us in her inimitable Russian accent to share her story with the world and to highlight her contribution to American acting training. So this is for Sonia Moore, as well as for those of us who studied with her and taught for her. *Spaseeba!*

Foreword

Whenever we gathered for a family dinner, my mother, Sonia Moore, would raise her glass to make her usual toast: "God Bless America." Sonia Moore had survived the Russian Revolution, the terror of Joseph Stalin, the constant fear for our lives, and the murder of our closest friends by Stalin and his henchmen.

My father was the head of the Soviet embassy in Rome, the acting ambassador, so we lived in palatial quarters with servants. The rest of the embassy staff was in tight, squalid quarters—a step up from Russian communal apartments. We lived in an environment where people would abruptly stop their conversations when anyone else, even their friends, approached within earshot. Children would cross the street to avoid other children whose father had been arrested or executed.

Having lived under that system, Sonia Moore simply was unable to trust anyone. The rest of her life would be affected by this terrible past. She felt unbounded gratitude, loyalty, and patriotism toward the United States, which had welcomed us and enabled us to lead safe lives. She respected and worshipped the democratic process.

We came to the United States with very little and had to struggle to survive. Since my father was a ranking Soviet diplomat and one of the earliest defectors, there were threats made on his life and fears that I might be kidnapped. Nonetheless, my father became a very successful businessman. Unhappily, soon after we were finally on our feet, my father was found to have cancer. For several years my mother's attention was totally focused on taking care of him. Her theatre interests took a back seat.

After his death, I encouraged her to begin teaching and helped her start a workshop in her apartment so that she could work on a play. Elliott Martin, who was then the production stage manager for a hit Broadway show in which I was acting, agreed to produce the play.

Sonia Moore had been an actress; however, teaching was her real calling. When I was in school, she was able to explain to me the most complicated subjects in the clearest, most concise terms. She wanted to see a theatre that would abandon the star system in favor of ensembles of technically trained, capable actors. She devoted the rest of her life—approximately forty years, or as long as it took Stanislavski to arrive at his ultimate technique, the Method of Physical Actions—to communicating Stanislavski's System to the American theatre through her books, lectures, classes, and teachers.

Unfortunately, her goal of an active school and a repertory company did not develop as she had hoped. She demanded control of every minute choice or decision, which led her to attend classes and correct instructors in the presence of the students. Instead of finding a theatre home where we could teach what she taught us, practice what we learned, and encourage others to join us in the pursuit of truth and artistic expression on stage, un-happily, we all had to leave.

Suzanne Trauth and Elizabeth Stroppel are wonderful examples of Sonia Moore's teaching. *Sonia Moore and American Acting Training: With a Sliver of Wood in Hand* shows that they thoroughly understand what Sonia Moore taught and who she was. By writing this book they have perpetuated her legacy. Their book is an honest and thorough documentary of Sonia Moore. I earnestly recommend this book as a must-read for theatre professionals and students.

—Irene Moore

Introduction

The greatest difficulty is to impress [on] the future actors that theatre is an important art. That theatre influences people. . . . Acting students must accept that they are on stage to reveal important thoughts in great plays. It is difficult because most students are satisfied to use a few clichés. It takes time but we do our best.[1]

—Sonia Moore

This hastily written note, dating from 1992, when Sonia Moore was ninety and three years away from the end of her life, succinctly summarizes her point of view on her years spent in the theatre: theatre is an essential, powerful institution, and actors need to learn discipline and patience to become true artists. All aspects of her theatrical life—from the way she ran her Studio to her rehearsal of plays—reflected this philosophy. The means to the end was the Stanislavski System.[2]

Sonia Moore's insistence that the Stanislavski System was the *only* path leading to the creation of this "important art" drew actors to her but also isolated her from some colleagues. As former students and teachers at the Sonia Moore Studio of the Theatre, we witnessed firsthand her passion for realizing her goals, as well as her struggle to overcome the resistance to her persistent efforts to promote Stanislavski.[3] She was mesmerizing in her belief and, at the same time, frustrating in her dogmatism.

Throughout the twentieth century and into the twenty-first, one of the most persistent arguments about actor training in the United States has set Lee Strasberg and the Actors Studio "Method" against Constantin Stanislavski's Russian "System." Strasberg's Americanized version of Stanislavski's System has focused, historically, on the actor's use of emotional memory through sense memory in the creation of character. Sonia Moore's first book, *The Stanislavski Method*, was written to counteract Strasberg's Method and to clarify Stanislavski's System. Its publication initiated her quest to train American actors in the System, particularly the Method of Physical Actions, a rehearsal process developed by Stanislavski during the last years of his life.[4] Through improvisation, the director and actors develop a logical sequence of physical actions. This sequence actively analyzes a play and its characters and simultaneously stimulates the psychological life of the actors. Through her subsequent books, the Sonia Moore Studio of the Theatre, the American Center for Stanislavski Theatre Art, the American Stanislavski Theatre, continuous research, lecturing, and workshops, Sonia Moore spent over three decades seeking ways to promote Stanislavski's legacy in the classroom and on the stage. In the process, she developed her own adaptation of the Method of Physical Actions that broadened the definition of physical action.

Moore operated in a world of contrasts. Her idealism about the potential influence of theatre went hand in hand with her realistic appraisal of her students. She loved the actors at her Studio even as she scolded them for being satisfied with ubiquitous clichés. Theatre was an event that could produce sweeping change, but performers needed to be reminded continually to "take their hands out of their pockets." Though time was a factor for Sonia Moore, since she did not embark on her career in the theatre in America until age fifty-eight, she was aware of the fact that mastering the Stanislavski System was a protracted affair. It required students' commitment well beyond the initial two years of study at her Studio.

Sonia Moore braved danger to escape the tyranny of Stalinist Russia, but in her Studio she often revealed her own authoritarian propensity. After her arrival in America, and afraid of what fate might have in store, she constantly carried a sliver of wood with her. When she needed to knock on wood for luck, it was always at hand: if she could not control the turmoil of life, she could at least be prepared to confront it.[5] Moore's life experiences may have bred a certain suspicion of others' motivations and a belief that she had to maintain control in order to survive and prosper. These characteristics permeated her teaching and directing. At opportune moments in the history of the Sonia Moore Studio, when relinquishing control might have given a degree of independence to students and faculty, she could not let go: the notion of a communal theatre reminded her of Soviet Russia.[6]

Moore wanted acceptance from the professional theatre world but rejected others' professional points of view. She got along best with those who agreed with her and who eagerly attempted to learn the lessons that she needed and wanted to teach. She adhered to her beliefs, though it caused students and faculty to leave the Studio. One of her former students recalled Sonia Moore's reference to her "bureau of disappointments," a fictional repository where she could "file away people and events that had upset her or disappointed her."[7] No one knows exactly how full, or how empty, the "bureau" was.

Former students also reported, with gratitude, that she had had a meaningful impact on their lives: she taught them aspects of acting technique they might not have learned elsewhere, she inspired them even when they were not certain about her process or experiments, and she provided a challenging, frustrating, exciting theatre experience.[8] Actor Vincent D'Onofrio stated that Sonia Moore taught him how to approach a role with discipline and how to find "the correct physical choices to help tell the story properly."[9]

Though she may not have achieved her intended goal of revolutionizing the American theatre, through her direct link to Stanislavski she played an important role in the history of the American theatre. Moore's tenacious efforts to promote Stanislavski in this country were unmatched by any in the theatre profession, and her death in May 1995 marked the end of an era. Her dedication to her students was such that on one of the coldest days of the winter just before her death, while she was still recuperating from a hospitalization, she supervised classes at the Studio.

In the process of writing this book, we drew on Sonia Moore's unpublished memoirs, provided by her daughter, Irene Moore; archival material gathered from private collections and from the New York Public Library for the Performing Arts; interviews with former teachers and students of the Studio; Stanislavski's books and texts that evaluate his System and its use and impact on American acting training; all of Moore's texts; and other literature on the history of acting training. We have included exercises from the Studio, and their use in model classes, to provide a glimpse into what was being taught at the time of Moore's passing.

Sonia Moore has been mentioned and referenced in research studies and analyses of Stanislavski's System in America, but to date there has been no in-depth study of her books, her Studio, or her place in the pantheon of acting teachers. This text attempts to fill that void. In retrospect, Moore might have been "tilting at windmills"[10] in her effort to reform American theatre, but her singleness of purpose garnered recognition and admiration from many.

ON A PERSONAL NOTE

I am a firm believer in the adage, "When the student is ready, the teacher appears." In the summer of 1986 I offered to replace a friend at a national theatre conference, to introduce Moore and to serve as chair of a panel discussion on "Sonia Moore and the Method of Physical Actions." When I called Sonia Moore and acquainted her with the change of events, she invited me to lunch at a quiet Italian restaurant on 57th Street, across from Carnegie Hall. I arrived promptly at the appointed time, entered the restaurant, and stepped into the dark interior. I was greeted by a young man who inquired if I needed a table for one. I explained that I was meeting a "Sonia Moore" for lunch, and immediately I was shown to a corner of the restaurant. She was seated against the back wall.

Her dress was simple, tasteful, and stylish. A colorful scarf was tied around her head, covering a long white braid pinned up underneath. Her remarkably expressive hands were decorated by several beautiful stones and her nails were meticulously painted. But it was her face that was most striking. As she shook my hand and invited me to join her at the table, I studied it. This face, both aged and ageless, projected a youthful vigor and liveliness. She was beautiful. Her eyes, masked and dilated by thick glasses that gave her a watery, emotional expression, absorbed my every movement. She was extraordinarily alert to every nuance of my behavior, and I felt as though I were being closely scrutinized.

At first, I was a little awestruck at meeting a legend of the theatre. I knew about her books and that she had studied under Evgeni Vakhtangov at the Third Studio of the Moscow Art Theatre. When I inquired about her work, she spoke of Stanislavski's final conclusions, the Method of Physical Actions, and, warming to her subject, lectured to me as I ate lasagna and she ignored her own meal. Her passion and lifelong commitment to Stanislavski were obvious.

I posed a few questions, but in general she needed little prompting to expand both on her own and Stanislavski's life's work. She inquired about my job at the university and nodded with a combination of approval and curiosity when I told her that I taught acting and directing. (Later I came to learn that she never really understood how anyone could teach those subjects effectively without having studied with her.) Lunch came to its conclusion and we still had not discussed the convention panel. She described her basic procedure—a brief talk followed by audience-participation exercises—and then she paid the bill for lunch, stifling my protests with few words and fewer gestures. Sonia Moore demonstrated great authority when checks were presented at the ends of meals.

We left the restaurant and stood outside under an overcast sky on the busy midday sidewalk. She wished me well, kissing me European-style on both cheeks, opened her umbrella, and began walking east on 57th Street after emphatically rejecting my suggestion of a cab. I reluctantly watched her depart, unwilling to let go of the afternoon's experience and unaware of what the future had in store for me. I felt that I had come in contact with history.

When I chaired the panel several months later, I became intrigued by Sonia Moore's discussion of psychophysical action and the use of the muscles along the spine. I thought that I understood Stanislavski's principles fairly well, as his work was the cornerstone of much of what I had taught in a variety of acting classes for over ten years. But this was a Stanislavski that I did not know. Many of my assumptions were challenged, and I wanted to re-think what I had been teaching so diligently during the prior decade.

Since I had a sabbatical approaching, I decided to take the following year off to study at the Sonia Moore Studio in New York. One year turned into eight years as I shifted from being a student to being both student and teacher at the Studio. Being a pupil of Sonia Moore was not always comfortable. I, like many students, felt crushed when admonished for not moving my muscles or choosing a gesture that satisfied her; frustrated when she made me reenter a scene again and again until I demonstrated the appropriate psychophysical involvement. But I was elated when she became excited about my work, when the physical and emotional aspects of the character came together and created something greater than the sum of the parts. Those moments are burned deeply into my memory.

I accompanied her to several theatre conventions over the years to contribute to panel discussions and to provide support for demonstrations of her technique. I witnessed the skepticism of some participants, but I also observed the hypnotic effect Sonia Moore had on many others. Her certainty when speaking about Stanislavski's System was captivating.

In addition to studying and teaching under her ever-vigilant eye, I performed the role of Beatrice in her final production of *A View from the Bridge*, served on the board of directors of the American Center for Stanislavski Theatre Art, and in the last years, assumed the position of assistant artistic director. In short, I immersed myself in Sonia Moore's work. It was an extraordinary journey, one of the most exhilarating and challenging experiences of my artistic life.

—Suzanne Trauth

As I sat writing the chapters of this book and listening to the words of former students and teachers, I reflected on my own ten-year journey under the guidance of Sonia Moore, an extraordinarily charming, intelligent, and at times exasperating woman. Not unlike others, it was through her books that I was initially attracted to her Studio. As an undergraduate, the first two texts on the study of acting that I encountered were Richard Boleslavsky's *Acting: The First Six Lessons* (1933) and Sonia Moore's *The Stanislavski System* (1965). Although I found Boleslavsky's text interesting, it seemed incomplete and difficult to translate into practice. In comparison, Moore's book intrigued me in a complete, hands-on way that simultaneously caused me to think critically about the art of acting because it was also so theoretically rich.

In 1979, after a class or two at other studios in New York City, I finally landed at the Sonia Moore Studio of the Theatre. After temping all day to pay the bills, I raced down the sidewalks of the city to the Studio's rented space in a church on West 57th Street. At times the church housed a few homeless people and international students; it continuously hosted support-group

meetings, such as Overeaters Anonymous. (One evening, I encountered co-
median Buddy Hackett in a darkened stairwell as he exited an Overeaters
Anonymous meeting, leaving me with a crude but somewhat funny memory
of the late comic.) Bursting with characters invaluable for a budding actor's
observations, and filled with sensations that often tested one's concentration,
I now realize how wide-eyed blind one had to be to commit to studying in
that locale with Moore. Nevertheless, many of us did, arriving from across
the country, the world, or even just the Hudson River, because we were so
eager to learn what she had to teach. After a year or so of study, I progressed
from student to beginning teacher. I found myself conflicted, though. I still
wanted to be an actor, a star! I continued to study and perform in the productions of the repertory company attached to the Studio, playing Natalya
Stepanovna in Chekhov's *The Marriage Proposal* and the brooding Charlotta
in *The Cherry Orchard*. Nevertheless, I did not feel particularly encouraged
by Moore in this endeavor. In suggesting that I start teaching, had she decided that my strength lay in sharing, in the classroom, what I had learned,
rather than in communicating a character's story to an audience from the
stage? A dispiriting thought at the time, I now realize how fortuitous the
move may have been for me. However, part of the reason I joined a splinter
group of the Studio in the mid-1980s was that I could continue to act with an
ensemble of similarly trained actors who were appreciative of my ability to
act as well as to teach.

What I did not realize when I saw Moore praising the acting of others yet
ignoring mine was that for Moore the ability to intellectualize a technique,
practice it, and then teach it was perhaps even more valuable than being able
to act. Actors could implement the technique in their performances, but
could they necessarily articulate what they did? Would others learn how to
practice the System simply by watching actors act?

Moore often felt betrayed when people moved on to act or study elsewhere. In her eyes, because she never finished speculating where
Stanislavski's work might have taken him if he had lived longer, her protégés
walked away with only partial knowledge. I left the Studio because I wanted
to study theatre academically and to teach at the university level. I believe that
she never forgave me for belonging to the theatre group formed by one of the
other teachers or for leaving my position as an instructor. From conversations
that we have conducted with former students, it is certain that a number of
people left the Studio on less-than-amiable terms with Moore. Moore's need
to hold on to students until they had learned all that she could discover was
not mean-spirited on her part but, perhaps, of an overreaching zeal.

—Elizabeth Stroppel

Whether or not you are familiar with Sonia Moore and her books, we hope
that this text will enable you to envision the dedicated teacher who quested

to give the adopted homeland that she loved one of the most treasured theatrical gifts her native Russia possessed: the Stanislavski System.

NOTES

1. This note is contained in the collection of Suzanne M. Trauth.

2. The *i* spelling of the name Stanislavski is chosen for this text, because when Sonia Moore wrote about him, it is the spelling she usually used. We have retained the *y* ending when it appears in other sources.

3. Dr. Stroppel was at the Studio from 1979 to 1988; Dr. Trauth was there from 1987 to 1995.

4. The capitalization of the term "Method of Physical Actions" acknowledges Sonia Moore's style when referring to it.

5. Irene Moore, interview by the authors, March 20, 2002. Irene Moore was twelve when her family defected from the Soviet Union. As an actor, she worked on and off Broadway, studied and taught at her mother's Studio, and performed in the repertory's productions. She currently teaches acting at New York University. Her perspective on Sonia Moore's life and work is invaluable.

6. Irene Moore, interview.

7. Linda S. Chapman, a former student of the Sonia Moore Studio, has remained a part of the New York theatre scene since she left the Studio in 1977. She has worked with such distinguished organizations as the Theater for the New City and the Wooster Group, and is currently the associate artistic director for the New York Theatre Workshop. Linda S. Chapman, interview by the authors, September 14, 2002.

8. From June 2002 until the present the authors interviewed a number of former students of the Sonia Moore Studio. Some of their responses are discussed in greater detail in chapter 5.

9. Vincent D'Onofrio, interview by the authors, January 17, 2005.

10. Dr. Felicia Londré, interview by the authors, June 27, 2002. Dr. Londré was a longtime friend and colleague of Sonia Moore. Currently, she is Curators' Professor of Theatre at the University of Missouri, Kansas City. When Londré received the 2001 Association for Theatre in Higher Education's Outstanding Teacher Award, she acknowledged Sonia Moore as a mentor.

1

Sonia Moore's Life: A Tale of Russian Intrigue and Determination

Sonia Moore was born December 4, 1902, to Evser and Sophie Shatzov in the provincial town of Gomel, Russia, located on a tributary of the Dnieper River. In "I Dared to Love, A Russian Memoir, 1917–1940,"[1] she describes her early life with her parents, two brothers, two sisters, a governess, and six servants in a two-story house topped with a little penthouse apartment Moore shared with her sisters.

Her family's house, the best in Gomel, was situated on a broad boulevard and surrounded by an orchard and a garden with a fountain and an oversized croquet set. In this idyllic setting she enjoyed a privileged existence with family and childhood friends, and her memoir provides vivid details of her life in the first decades of the twentieth century. Advantages such as indoor plumbing, a staff of servants to tend to the family's needs, a storehouse of fine foods, and a surplus of fine fabrics and jewelry, purchased as a result of her mother's fondness for buying goods in large quantities, indicate Moore's family's wealth. Moore's memoir also eloquently reveals both the excitement and the trauma of making her debut at age fourteen. When singled out by a mysterious admirer and dubbed "the queen of the ball," she was ushered dramatically into adulthood.[2] A succession of young and not-so-young men pursued the youthful Moore while she fretted over Pavel, with whom she thought she was in love and who eventually became her first husband.

The romantic interludes of her adolescence, however, were shaped significantly by the political undercurrents of the revolution that dominated Gomel during the last years of World War I. With the rise of the Communist Party and talk of insurrection, survival became precarious for members of the bourgeoisie. The possibility of banishment, the anarchist Red and

1

counterrevolutionary White armies battling at various times for control of the city, and sudden, unexplained arrests all lent an atmosphere of uncertainty to this period of her life. The picture of Sonia Moore that emerges from her memoir of these early years is that of a somewhat sheltered young woman who was shy, almost speechless, when confronted with potential suitors. Yet she was simultaneously curious about the world beyond Gomel and the political implications of choices made by family members and friends. When faced with danger, she was unexpectedly calm under pressure. Whether deceiving soldiers to secure her safety or scrubbing floors for the first time in her life to create a livable home in exile, Moore demonstrated her resourcefulness and courage.

By 1917 life was changing quickly. Moore's education gradually came to an end at the fifth level—three classes short of graduation from high school. By the time of the October Revolution, her father thought it best to move the family to Kiev, where they were unknown and his affluence would not prove to be a liability. Some of the rooms in their house were already being requisitioned by a Communist's family.[3] Moore's father, mother, and sisters left for Kiev while Moore remained behind with her older brother's family to care for her three-year-old brother, who was stricken with scarlet fever.

The unpredictable terror and melodrama of those tempestuous times is evident in her description of a particular incident. When authorities threatened to expel Gomel's bourgeoisie, Moore's older brother left for Moscow to obtain permission to remain in the village. One day, while he was gone, she and her sister-in-law were ordered by Russian soldiers to accompany them to sign papers. On their way home they were arrested by two other soldiers and escorted to Lubianka prison, where they waited hours to discover why they had been taken into custody. Finally, Sasha, a seventeen-year-old Red Army soldier and one of Moore's admirers, "burst in waving two guns in his hands and when asked for a pass, he shook his guns and said, 'Here is my pass.'" Having been wrongly arrested, they were released immediately.[4]

As Sonia Moore and her sister-in-law prepared to leave Gomel without her older brother, they were subjected to searches so thorough that "the soles of our only pair of shoes were ripped apart." Exiled to the village of Propoisk, where they lived in two rooms, Moore tired of her oppressive existence and decided to escape. With her little brother in her arms and her sister-in-law following behind, she braved local police, defied the order of exile, and boarded a boat to return to Gomel. In each of her shipmates she saw a "secret agent of the CHEKA [KGB]."[5] Upon arrival, she discovered that her brother had obtained permits allowing them to reside in Gomel legally. Shortly after, they packed and left on a boat for Kiev.

Since her studies at the Gymnazia in Gomel were incomplete, Moore found a tutor and a few months later gained admission to a Kiev high school. Throughout this period, the revolution raged around her family. From the window of their small house she watched soldiers fall lifelessly as the Red Army fought the White Army on the square below. The moaning of the wounded was mingled with the screams of her mother urging her to move away from the window, fearful that a stray bullet would kill her. But she was mesmerized by her view of the armies at war and the frightening sights she witnessed. Later, Moore wondered if she knew intuitively that somewhere in the Red Army was a young soldier with whom she would share both happy and unfortunate experiences in the years to come.[6]

During the civil war, Kiev was occupied by a variety of political groups, including Ukrainian Nationalists and Poles, as well as the White and Red armies. The year Moore graduated from high school, thirteen different armies controlled Kiev at various times. On the night of her graduation, Poles were in charge and her diploma was a Polish one, which was more valuable than a Soviet diploma. By the time the graduation party ended early the next morning, the Red Army was again in control.[7]

Meanwhile, Moore's father was in negotiations with Polish Prince Radzivil to purchase the prince's apartment in a wealthier part of Kiev, the fashionable Passage on Kreschatic Street. As they were preparing to move to their new home, Moore witnessed horrifying incidents. From her window she watched as a plundering band of Chechens marched from house to house, looting and beating the inhabitants. Worse still, the White Army, under the command of General Denikin, began to systematically slaughter Jewish citizens of Kiev. The moment his troops entered a house, the people would scream to warn neighbors that they were being attacked, in hopes of allowing some inhabitants to escape. As the marauders moved down the street, a "relay of screams" moved as well. Moore recalled that she awoke to unusual sounds emanating from far off. What seemed at first to be moaning within a short time swelled to a terrifying howling that could be heard in every part of Kiev. This "human siren" poured from hundreds of Jewish victims.[8]

Though many in the city who had previously celebrated the exit of the Red Army now wished for its return, Sonia Moore's father disagreed. He was a stubborn man who resisted the notion of the Bolsheviks in power and felt that the revolution and the rise of the Communist Party were transitory events.

After graduating from high school, Moore entered the Drama School of the State Solovtzov Theatre and also enrolled at Kiev University to study biology. At about that time, she heard that Pavel had been arrested in Moscow. Influenced by romantic stories of Russian heroines, and over the vehement objections of her parents, she slept for five nights in the boxcar of a freight train to join him in Moscow. Because he had already been released from jail and was in no imminent danger, she returned to Kiev sorry for having worried her parents.[9] Still, it was obvious that, even as a young girl, she confronted danger head-on, regardless of the consequences.

At this time, her family was planning its emigration from Russia to Latvia. As a result of new laws implemented after World War I, Soviets born in Latvia, Lithuania, or Estonia, all new independent states, could claim citizenship and return to their land of birth. Moore's sister-in-law was Latvian, and it seemed the perfect opportunity for the family to move abroad. Because it was not without risk since documents had to be forged, her father resisted the idea of leaving Russia forever, but he was finally persuaded, and preparations to leave were begun. Moore, however, informed her family that she intended to marry Pavel in Moscow. Though she expected her father to prevent her from leaving the family, she was surprised to hear him say, "Whatever is destined to be, just be. Your life must run its perhaps stormy course."[10] She acknowledged later that had her father insisted, she would have left with the family. But he did not, so she remained in Russia and married Pavel, in her own words a "disastrous event." She was sixteen.

THE THIRD STUDIO

For a time, Sonia Moore studied biology in the Department of Natural Sciences at the University of Moscow, but life was extremely trying for the newlyweds. Occupying one room in a shared apartment and struggling to make ends meet, since Pavel's salary from working in a bookstore was insufficient, for several months they survived only on barley cooked in water. Pavel was arrested again, and it was three weeks before the authorities realized they had made a mistake. During this period, time passed slowly and the days were boring, broken only by the occasional outing, such as visits to a café that had become a meeting place for young Soviet writers. She remembered incomprehensible poetry by avant garde celebrities delivered to the applause of an enthusiastic crowd. She felt, however, that "an unwholesome atmosphere reigned among the Russian intelligenzia."[11]

Moore had forgotten her father's admonition to do something useful for others and for oneself every day. Restless and yearning to tend to her spiritual needs, she reached out to an acquaintance who encouraged her to audition for the Kamerny Theatre. Under the tutelage of Vigilev, an actor from the Kamerny, she began work on Oscar Wilde's *Salome* and Leonid Andreev's *The Life of a Man* in preparation for the highly competitive and rigorous auditions.

The Kamerny Theatre was known for beautiful movement and voice; consequently, her coaching consisted of lowering and raising her voice on certain lines and of creating acrobatic, stylized movement.[12] When friends from the drama school in Kiev suddenly arrived in Moscow, intending to audition for the Third Studio of the Moscow Art Theatre, which was under the direction of Evgeni Vakhtangov, and for the Chekhov Studio, headed by Michael

Chekhov, they persuaded Moore to join them. It was all the encouragement she needed. With only ten days remaining until the examinations, she had to apply herself seriously.

On the day of the audition for the Chekhov Studio, Sonia Moore found herself in a room with two actors and Chekhov himself. She presented the character of Salome and, according to the custom for such auditions, recited a fable and performed an improvisation. Her friend, the next person called into the room, overheard Chekhov say, "They are beginning to come to us from the Kamerny. Let us accept her." Upon hearing this news, Moore almost decided to cancel her audition for the Third Studio.

There were 560 applicants to the Moscow Art Theatre's Third Studio, and preliminary auditions were conducted by actors of the Studio. Sonia Moore was one of fifty-seven actors admitted for the final audition in front of Vakhtangov. Though overjoyed at the news, she did think "it might have been better to have failed the preliminary test than to have to go through all the torture again."[13]

Because Vakhtangov was performing that night, the audition did not begin until after eleven o'clock in the evening. When he arrived, there was a murmur in the large waiting room and then silence. The audition began. At three o'clock in the morning, and after hearing Vakhtangov berate previous auditionees, Sonia Moore wanted to leave. Instead, she entered the small studio with trepidation, and he ordered her to read the part of Salome. She started, using the acrobatic gestures Vigilev taught her, and had just reached the climactic moment when Vakhtangov cut her off. Though she feared the worst, he simply found her work to that point sufficient. He queried her about her home, and when she informed him that she was not from Moscow but had come from Kiev the previous year, he was surprised at her lack of accent. No one entering the Moscow Art Theatre was permitted to have any accent but the Moscow Russian of the poet Aleksandr Pushkin. Later, Vakhtangov was heard saying, "There was one girl from Kiev we accepted. Not the slightest accent."[14] Sonia Moore attributed her "miraculously acquired Moscow accent as a gift from God in preparation for her future mission."[15]

As one of only fourteen actors chosen to enter the Third Studio during that audition process, she began a regimen in 1920 that lasted for several years. She related tales of all-night rehearsals directed by Vakhtangov that began after the performance of whatever play he was acting in at the time, and uncompromising discipline in the training of the actors. Daytime hours were consumed with classes, as well as with other duties such as sewing, painting, dusting, and scrubbing. She attacked all of it with an insatiable desire to learn. Both Constantin Stanislavski, cofounder of the Moscow Art Theatre, and Vakhtangov considered the theatre a family of actors who were dedicating their lives to art.[16] Apparently, her only conflict at the Studio involved her desire to play character parts when she was "forced to study romantic roles." Because she persisted in her demand, she was brought before the Studio's Art Council to determine if she had the necessary sense of comedy to play character roles. All members but one decided that she had.[17]

Vakhtangov began rehearsal for a production of *Princess Turandot*, though he was seriously ill and was assumed to be suffering from cancer, because he often grasped his side in pain or left the rehearsal hall for a time. But he would not give up his work. The preview date of *Princess Turandot* had been set, and Vakhtangov directed the final rehearsal "in a dressing gown with a compress on his head."[18] The following day was the run-through for the Moscow Art Theatre and its Studios; Vakhtangov, however, was too sick to attend and never again left his bed. Stanislavski visited him during the intermission to congratulate him on the extraordinary success of the production, calling it a work of magnificence and genius. Vakhtangov's beliefs that every play demanded its own unique form and every character its own clear, distinct pattern were evident in his production of *Princess Turandot*. Later that night Stanislavski wrote Vakhtangov a letter suggesting that in his time with the Moscow Art Theatre there had been few such victories as *Turandot*.[19] Vladimir Nemirovich-Danchenko, Stanislavski's artistic partner at the Moscow Art Theatre, proclaimed that Vakhtangov had achieved a great triumph by infusing traditional aspects of Stanislavski's System of actor training with new stylistic elements. He applauded Vakhtangov's efforts to honor his roots with the Moscow Art Theatre while dissolving the bonds of a "grey and boring Naturalism."[20]

The high excitement of opening night was temporary because everyone knew that Vakhtangov was dying. Sonia Moore recalled how Studio members paid visits to his apartment, sitting in an adjoining room and hoping to catch a glimpse of their beloved teacher. Moore was able to offer him some aid during this time. Vakhtangov's illness required that he eat certain foods difficult to obtain in Moscow, and Moore, though wary about making contact with her family abroad, wired them anyway and requested they send the specific provisions that he needed. When the food arrived she delivered it to his wife.[21]

After lingering for three months, Vakhtangov died May 29, 1922, surrounded by his students and colleagues. His death devastated the theatre community of Moscow. Moore remembered weeping inconsolably as she sat on the steps leading up to his apartment. All of the celebrated actors of the Moscow Art Theatre paid homage at his funeral, and Vakhtangov's wife led a pale Michael Chekhov by the hand to the casket. Sonia Moore recalled Vakhtangov's "sparkling, ironical humor, his sharp intelligence, artistic sense, limitless energy, and . . . hatred of all that was vulgar." She noted that on occasions when his work proved to be dissatisfying, Vakhtangov would suddenly abandon work that had been accomplished during long nights of rehearsal.[22] Moore "worshipped Vakhtangov" and was "in absolute awe of him."[23] With his death, she felt that her ties to the world of theatre had been weakened.

She continued for a time at the Studio, replacing one of the actresses in *Princess Turandot* who had fallen ill. Sonia Moore remembered feeling deeply moved when she played on the stage of the Moscow Art Theatre.[24] By 1923, however, her interest was waning and she quit the Studio. She admitted that she did poorly on her examination and had lost confidence in the Third Studio now that Vakhtangov was no longer its leader.[25] Perhaps most importantly, in 1923 she met Lev Borisovich Helfand (he later changed his name to Leon Moore), the son of a Ukrainian landowner, who had joined the Red Army at age seventeen as an act of idealism and eventually rose to the rank of general. His handsome face and commanding presence mesmerized her, and she fell in love. Though the attraction was mutual, Moore insisted on remaining loyal to her husband and resisted Helfand's attentions.[26] When at last she divorced Pavel, Helfand became her second husband.

A NEW LIFE

While Sonia Moore was living and studying in Moscow, her family remained in Riga, Latvia, where she visited them in 1923. Her father, convinced that the Soviet regime would collapse and they would be able to return to Russia, decided not to use the American visas that he had obtained. After a series of strokes, he died in 1928. With the exception of Moore, an older sister, and her older brother, the remainder of the family perished in Nazi concentration camps during World War II.[27]

Also in 1923, Moore went to Berlin to work as an actress with the Russian Theatre. For three years she successfully avoided Helfand, but he finally persuaded her to accompany him to Paris, where he was posted to gain diplomatic experience, first as vice consul at the Soviet General Consulate and later as second secretary. Following her divorce, Sonia Moore married Helfand in May 1926 in Paris, and their daughter Irene was born in April 1928. Moore earned a diploma in French at the Alliance Française and learned "how to function as a diplomat's wife."[28]

In 1930 the Helfands found themselves back in Moscow, where Lev Borisovich worked in the Commissariat for Foreign Affairs. During this period, Moore, though primarily a wife and mother, attended performances at all of the major theatres, including all of the productions directed by Vsevolod Meyerhold and Alexander Tairov.[29]

In 1935, during the Stalinist purges, they were sent to Rome, where they were to remain until they defected to the United States in 1940. Moore earned an additional diploma from the Instituto Interuniversitario Italiano and degrees from the Reale Conservatorio di Musica Santa Cecilia and the Reale Accademia Filarmonica. The Helfands were counting on Moore giving Italian and voice lessons in the United States to help support the family. For four years they planned their departure while she saved money, ran the Intourist travel agency in Rome, and worked as a singing teacher to help cover their travel expenses across the Atlantic.

In 1940, when they were scheduled to return to Russia, the Helfands packed their belongings and sent them home. But instead of following, they escaped from Italy with the help of U.S. secretary of state Cordell Hull and the American ambassador William Phillips. At the time of their defection, Lev Borisovich Helfand was Chargé d'Affaires of the Soviet embassy in Rome and Soviet representative to the League of Nations in Geneva.[30]

The disturbing events of the days before and during the defection were traumatic. Sonia Moore admitted that "her inner panic while attempting to keep up a good front at the Embassy caused her to pack irrationally, so that family treasures were sent to Moscow . . . while useless items were carried on the flight." The deception included the family's public exit from Rome by train and a clandestine return to Rome later that evening. After spending a number of hours concealed in the apartment of an American correspondent, the family escaped on the "one daily flight from Rome to Lisbon via Barcelona and Madrid."[31]

Nearly penniless when they arrived in New York, it was suggested that Leon Moore, as he was now called, drive a taxi to help support the family. An economist by education, he eventually became very successful in the coal and oil industry, while Sonia Moore gave singing lessons and kept busy creating a new life in the United States. President Truman signed a special bill granting the Moores citizenship, shortening the normal amount of time required for a former Communist Party member to become a citizen.[32] Though they left the material aspects of their lives behind in Rome and Moscow, their spirits were encouraged by the move. Sadly, seven years after they arrived in America, Leon became ill and, after a long battle with cancer, died in 1957.

A RETURN TO THE THEATRE

For a number of years Sonia Moore remained outside the theatre, choosing instead to devote her time and energy to her family. Devastated by the loss of her spouse of thirty-one years, she found herself unable to cope, by her own account barely functioning. While visiting her brother in England, she had begun to recover when he suffered a heart attack and needed her help to pull through. During this trip she somehow found a book on Stanislavski in her lap on the plane. Though she later claimed not to have known how it got there, the book apparently rekindled her passion for theatre, and an article in the *New York Times* about the American Method sparked her active return to it.

NOTES

1. Sonia Moore, "I Dared to Love, A Russian Memoir, 1917–1940," unpublished manuscript, 1994, collection of Irene Moore.
2. Moore, "I Dared to Love," 8–10.
3. *World Biographical Hall of Fame*, rev. ed. (Raleigh, N.C.: Historical Preservations of America, 1992), s.v. "Moore, Sonia": 4:1–7.
4. *World Biographical Hall of Fame*, 1.
5. *World Biographical Hall of Fame*, 1.
6. *World Biographical Hall of Fame*, 2.
7. *World Biographical Hall of Fame*, 2.
8. *World Biographical Hall of Fame*, 2.
9. *World Biographical Hall of Fame*, 2–3.
10. *World Biographical Hall of Fame*, 3.
11. *World Biographical Hall of Fame*, 4.
12. Moore, "I Dared to Love," 93.
13. Moore, "I Dared to Love," 96.
14. Moore, "I Dared to Love," 100.
15. Felicia Londré, "Sonia Moore," unpublished manuscript, 1981: 1, collection of Felicia Londré.
16. Moore, "I Dared to Love," 100.
17. Moore, "I Dared to Love," 101.
18. Moore, "I Dared to Love," 103.
19. Moore, "I Dared to Love," 104.
20. Moore, "I Dared to Love," 104.
21. Moore, "I Dared to Love," 105.
22. Sonia Moore, *The Stanislavski System* (New York: Penguin, 1984), 86.
23. Irene Moore, interview by the authors, March 20, 2002.
24. Moore, "I Dared to Love," 106.
25. Moore, "I Dared to Love," 114.
26. Felicia Hardison Londré, "Stanislavski's Champion: Sonia Moore and Her Crusade to Save the American Theatre," *Theatre History Studies* 24 (June 2004): 17.
27. Londré, "Stanislavski's Champion," 17.
28. Londré, "Stanislavski's Champion," 17.
29. Londré, "Stanislavski's Champion," 17.
30. *World Biographical Hall of Fame*, 5.
31. Londré, "Stanislavski's Champion," 18.
32. Irene Moore, interview.

2

Sonia Moore's Context: Professional Acting Training in New York City

Unlike other Russian theatrical artists who continued to perform and teach after immigrating to America, Sonia Moore remained in the theatrical wings.[1] When she did insert herself publicly into the theatre scene in New York City in the late 1950s, Stalin was dead, condemned as a murderer in 1956 by Nikita Khrushchev. A guarded cultural exchange existed with Russia. In 1958, for example, as the Moscow Art Theatre celebrated its sixtieth anniversary, the New York Public Library assembled a tribute to Constantin Stanislavski.[2]

At that time also, interest in the craft of acting was particularly high, stirred by competing studios and the sparks that flew over interpretations of Stanislavski's technique that had filtered into the United States in the 1920s. In July 1957 the *New York Times* proclaimed that theatre had regained its vigor, having the busiest season since the 1920s, driven by, among other elements, "a larger and more professional cadre of actors" than any other period in history.[3] Controversy escalated around Strasberg's Method, as actors from the Actors Studio became progressively more successful in films and on stage, and others in the industry opposed what appeared to be a distortion of Stanislavski's System.

In a December 8, 1957, interview of actor Anthony Perkins entitled "Triumph of Nature over Method," a young Perkins admitted surprise at his success on Broadway and in films, and an intense fear of studying how to act since he had never taken a single lesson:

> Sometimes actors talk to me about methods and training and all of a sudden, I get a terrible chill. I don't know what they're talking about. I'm afraid to start studying now, just as some actors are afraid of analysis—they fear it will change them. I'm really on treacherous ground.[4]

It was this article that provoked Sonia Moore into action. She told writer Herbert Kupferberg in a later interview, "That was when I realized that Stanislavski's method was not properly understood in the United States."[5] Moore responded quickly to the Perkins interview by sending the following letter to Brooks Atkinson, drama critic of the *New York Times*:

> For a long time Stanislavsky's Method has been discussed by many theatrical personalities and subjected to varied and sometimes highly critical opinions. . . . I was a member of the Vakhtangov Theatre in Moscow, which is also known as the Third Studio of the Moscow Art Theatre. Consequently, I studied under K. S. Stanislavsky and the great actor and great director, E. B. Vakhtangov whom Stanislavsky considered his best pupil and who, Stanislavsky said, taught his Method better than he himself. . . .
>
> Stanislavsky never meant his Method to compete with Nature. . . . The Method was created by Stanislavsky in order to help nature as he believed that only a few have the talent such as Anthony Perkins of "Look Homeward Angel" has. With [the] Method, Stanislavsky wanted to help actors to do what Mr. Perkins and other exceptionally talented actors and actresses do subconsciously. Mr. Perkins should not be afraid to acquaint himself with the Method because he will find out that he is doing just what Stanislavsky taught actors to do. So [do] Helen Hayes and other excellent actors who do not use the Method.[6]

In this letter Moore implied that she was aware of the controversy in the profession surrounding Stanislavski's System. She also proclaimed that she was personally experienced in the System, and could, therefore, speak knowledgeably about it. Anecdotally, Atkinson then encouraged Moore to write a book about Stanislavski's technique, to help clarify some of the common misconceptions. A few years later, *The Stanislavski Method* (1960) was published. By the time Sonia Moore wrote her letter to the *New York Times*, Russian influence on American acting training was already well established.

THE TRADITION OF ACTING TRAINING IN AMERICA

To this day, the most acclaimed genesis of contemporary acting training in the United States is Stanislavski's System.[7] In 1923 and 1924 Constantin Stanislavski and his Moscow Art Theatre (MAT) performed in New York City and in other cities across the United States.[8] The MAT's realistic portrayals and ensemble effort excited audiences. "Aspects of the company's work most often praised included the actors' seamless portrayal of character; their creation of an illusion of real life without obvious theatricality but with clear artistry."[9] This contrasted starkly with the unrealistic, star attitude exhibited by American-trained actors on the commercial stage. A clamor for

Stanislavski's technique resulted as young actors and directors "watched as if the secret to great theatre were being offered to them. They longed to learn to act in this way, to create the same kind of theatre in their own idiom."[10] Russians from the MAT taught Stanislavski's work at existing studios and also opened their own, eclipsing the lessons taught in American acting schools.[11]

The story of Stanislavski's triumphant presentation of the MAT is well documented, as is the resulting demand for his acting system.[12] For decades theatre historians have traced the lineage of prominent twentieth-century acting teachers in America to Stanislavski. Although Russian actors associated with the MAT, such as Alla Nazimova, had performed in this country as early as 1905, Richard Boleslavsky and Maria Ouspenskaya are credited with being the first to begin teaching in a formalized setting, the American Lab Theatre in New York City in late 1923.[13] A host of aspiring actors and directors, such as Stella Adler, Lee Strasberg, and Harold Clurman, took classes from Boleslavsky and Ouspenskaya. These actors and others who studied with them became some of the most influential theatrical figures in the United States.

In 1931 Clurman, along with Cheryl Crawford and Elia Kazan, also former students at the Lab Theatre, began the Group Theatre, a collective of young, idealistic actors, directors, and playwrights who produced plays with social impact as the Depression ravaged the country.[14] Through their ensemble effort and experimentation with Stanislavski's acting process, the Group took on the role of America's version of the Moscow Art Theatre. It is revered as the most significant theatre in U.S. acting history, in spite of the fact that "its failures are more easily assessed than its successes."[15] Famous artists, such as actor Franchot Tone and playwright Clifford Odets, emerged from this group. In 1941, ten years after its inception, the Group Theatre disbanded because of artistic differences and commitments to Hollywood. Most importantly for acting training in this country, however, ex-members taught what they had learned as part of the Group and/or continued to practice their art, developing their own interpretations of Stanislavski's System.

A number of the former Group members began studios that still thrive today. Stella Adler, for example, created the Stella Adler Conservatory of Theatre in 1947. Adler based her interpretation of Stanislavski's work on imagination, circumstances, and action.[16] At the Actors Studio, originally founded in 1947 for actors to have a place to practice and develop their craft, Lee Strasberg became the dominant figure. Sanford Meisner was affiliated with the Neighborhood Playhouse School of Theatre, a school that grew out of the defunct Neighborhood Playhouse in 1928. At that institution, Meisner developed his emphasis on spontaneous communication with partners.[17]

OTHER RUSSIAN ACTING TEACHERS

In addition to Boleslavsky and Ouspenskaya, other former students of Stanislavski and members of the MAT had immigrated to New York City and elsewhere, creating studios and teaching in existing schools. The most well known is Michael Chekhov (1896–1955). Chekhov is reputed to have been Stanislavski's most successful pupil in terms of his own acting talents. In the United States, he taught at the Chekhov Theatre Studio in Connecticut until 1941, the Chekhov New York Theatre Studio until World War II forced it to close in 1942, and then in Hollywood, on and off, until his death in 1955. Most of his time, however, was spent in Europe.[18] Lee Strasberg, Stella Adler, and others studied briefly with Chekhov in the 1930s, but Chekhov's impact on American acting through his teaching has not been as proclaimed as the brilliance of his own performance abilities.[19] His books *To the Actor* (1953), revised in 1991 and retitled *On the Technique of Acting,* and *Lessons for the Professional Actor* (1985), a collection of exercises and lectures from his New York studio from 1941, illuminate his take on acting.[20] Since the 1980s, the interest in Chekhov's work has continued to grow, especially with the opening of the Michael Chekhov Studio in New York City in 1980 by Beatrice Straight and Robert Cole.[21]

Other notable former members of the MAT in addition to Chekhov also taught in Manhattan: Tamara Daykarhanova (c.1889–1980); Barbara (n.d.) and Leo Bulgakov (1899–1948); Vera Soloviova (1891–1986) and Andrius Jilinsky (d. 1948); and Miriam Goldina (1898–1979). Collectively, these émigrés instructed American students from the late 1920s into the early 1970s. In addition, they also influenced theatre in this country through their performing, directing, producing, writing, and translating skills.[22] While they taught in places such as the American Theatre Wing and the Neighborhood Playhouse, all of them eventually established their own studios. A number of them also attempted to put together theatre troupes. Jilinsky is the only one of this group who has a book about acting published in his name.[23]

Daykarhanova began the Studio of Stage Make-Up in 1929 with another former MAT actor, Akim Tamiroff (1899–1972). She also taught for Ouspenskaya.[24] In 1935 she founded her own school, Daykarhanova's School for the Stage, which included a comprehensive program of drama, voice and speech, body technique, stage make-up, costume, singing, and dramatic interpretation of song. The school was most active in the 1930s and the 1940s, with a thriving summer program in Westchester County, north of New York City. It lasted until 1971 under the codirectorship of a former pupil, Hollywood director Joseph Anthony. Anthony used the studio to recruit actors for his films, not unlike the way in which Elia Kazan benefited from the Group Theatre. Daykarhanova's biography in one of the brochures for her school states, "Ever since she first came to this country (1921), she has devoted herself to the demands and ideals of the American theatre."[25] Evidently, Daykarhanova was one of the most prominent and lasting members of the MAT to spread Stanislavski's teachings in New York. She did not, however, write any texts.

Leo and Barbara Bulgakov both succeeded in this country as performers after staying behind when the MAT returned to Russia. Leo was also a passionate director and producer. The Bulgakovs taught in various places and in 1931 opened the Westchester Repertory Company. In 1939 they founded the Bulgakov Studio of Theatre Art, which closed in 1942.[26] The *New York Times* obituary for Leo noted that as a former member of the MAT, he tried to establish a repertory theatre in America "which would command respect for its artistic excellence," but never could because of a lack of funds.[27] Barbara continued to teach her husband's classes at the American Theatre Wing until the late 1950s. She also taught at Daykarhanova's school.[28]

The wife-and-husband team of Vera Soloviova and Andrius Jilinsky had toured with the MAT in America and returned to Russia upon finishing an assignment in Lithuania. After a stint with Michael Chekhov in Paris, they returned to New York in 1935 with Chekhov's Moscow Art Players.[29] They instructed at Daykarhanova's studio for five years in the mid-1930s before Jilinsky began the New York Troupe. In 1938 he formed the American Actors Company with graduates of Daykarhanova's school, and in 1940 they opened the Actor's Workshop. They also taught at the Mildred Gellendré Studio in the mid-1940s, which became Jilinsky's Acting Studio. After her husband died in 1948, Soloviova continued to teach. In 1951 she opened the Vera Soloviova Studio, which lasted into the 1960s.

Miriam Goldina had studied at Vakhtangov's Third Studio, as Sonia Moore had, and arrived in the United States with the Habima Theatre in 1929.[30] She taught in New York, opening her own studio in 1940, the year that Sonia Moore arrived in the United States, and taught in Hollywood as well. She acted and directed and served as artistic director of the Acting Lab at Bryn Mawr College and the Greenwich Mews Theatre in New York City. Goldina also taught as an associate professor at the University of Florida, worked with various other theatres, and made guest appearances on television. Although she did not write any books, she did translate two important texts, *Stanislavsky Directs* by Nikolai M. Gorchakov (1954) and *Stanislavsky's Protégé: Eugene Vakhtangov* by Rubin Simonov (1969). Goldina continued to leave her mark on American theatre until her death in 1979.

On February 2, 1958, Arthur Gelb published an interview with Barbara Bulgakov in the *New York Times*, just one month after the letter from Sonia Moore had appeared.[31] In that article, Gelb claimed that only five people who acted with Stanislavski's MAT resided in America at that time. Besides Bulgakov, Gelb named Daykarhanova, Soloviova, Akim Tamiroff, and Olga

Baclanova (1899–1974).[32] Gelb's statement was clearly limited by his estima-
tion that the Russians named were the only "qualified proponents" to defend
Stanislavski's theories against the "mocking public scrutiny" generated by the
American Method controversy. Absent from this list of known
teachers/artists were Goldina, who had been visible in America for decades,
and Sonia Moore, who had just made her presence known. Although neither
of these women had toured with the MAT, they had studied at Vakhtangov's
Third Studio and possessed authentic knowledge of the System.

THE METHOD CONTROVERSY

In 1964 Paul Gray wrote that the first MAT actors to come to this country and
spread Stanislavski's work began thinning in the 1950s.[33] Commending
Soloviova and Daykarhanova for still bringing their significant lessons to students, he also observed that, as the number of students dwindled, teaching
had become for the Russians "a matter of coaching alone, separated from
theatrical productions."[34] Gray's comments imply that America's fascination
with the original Russian influence on acting training had passed its heyday,
and now American reinterpretations prevailed. Indeed, the efforts of the Russian émigrés to continue to disseminate Stanislavski's technique in this country as they had learned it seemed to have been eclipsed by the efforts of former members of the Group Theatre.[35]

Yet it was at this period that Sonia Moore started to make her mark on acting training in this country through her books, Sonia Moore Studio of the
Theatre, and the American Center for Stanislavski Theatre Art. In looking
back, it would seem that part of her success, and part of her failure, had to
do with this timing.

There is no doubt that at the Actors Studio, the Method became the gospel
for scores of actors into the 1950s. With its emphasis on emotional and sense
memory, intimately revealing exercises such as "Private Moments," and the
psychoanalytical probing that Strasberg put actors through to unravel their
own complexities as human beings, Strasberg became legendary and caused
controversy.[36] He referred to his version of Stanislavski's work as distinct
from Stanislavski's in a letter to Christine Edwards for her 1965 text *The
Stanislavsky Heritage*:

> I do not believe that anyone has a right to talk of the Stanislavsky System. I have
> therefore stressed the use of the word "Method" as against "System" to suggest
> that while we obviously are influenced by Stanislavsky's ideas and practices, we
> used it within the limitations of our own knowledge and experience. . . .
>
> In other words, while it would be true to say that we try to make use of the
> basic ideas of the Stanislavsky System, we do not feel it necessary to be limited
> just to those ideas or procedures. . . .

I therefore think it theoretically wise and practically sound to talk of the work done by the Group Theatre and the Actors Studio as being an "Adaptation of the Stanislavsky System." The "Method" is therefore our version of the System.[37]

As successful as the Method proved to be for some actors, especially those performing in film, resistance came from a number of sources because of its apparent self-indulgent dominance of actor over character. Battles were fought in newspapers and journals throughout the 1950s. In 1956 a flurry of articles appeared in the *New York Times*. Seymour Peck's "The Temple of 'The Method'" painted a picture of the Actors Studio as hallowed ground, although not without cracks, as he detailed, for example, the harsh personal criticism that Strasberg leveled at students.[38] Still, when Peck interviewed members of the Actors Studio, such as Shelley Winters and Kim Stanley, they praised the Method and Strasberg. Jack Gould followed Peck's article with one in which he denounced the introspective acting being promoted by the Actors Studio to be "psychological gymnastics behind closed doors. . . . To stimulate one's own emotions on stage is mere child's play in comparison with the artistry required to simulate the emotions of an altogether different person created by the author."[39] A week later, nine letters were printed in the Drama Mailbag section, most in agreement with Gould on the type of therapeutic, stylistically monotonous, and self-contained acting that people associated with the Actors Studio.[40]

In September 1956 Lee Strasberg wrote an article entitled "View from the Studio." In it, he defended his Method against the myths surrounding it, and again, trumpeted its originality from the System.[41] Two weeks later, five letters in the Drama Mailbag responded to Strasberg's article, four vitriolic ones against the "aesthetic snobs" that the Actors Studio appeared to be promoting.[42] In April 1957 director/teacher Robert Lewis held his now-famous series of Monday night talks entitled "Method—or Madness?" to clarify points about the System. He gave theatrical professionals a chance to ask questions openly about differences between Stanislavski's System and the Method. Lewis then wrote an article for the *New York Times* about the lectures, as well as a book with the same title as the lecture series. Of Lewis's 1958 text, Edwards wrote:

> It is a lucid statement of the principles underlying the Stanislavsky System and should certainly silence the carpers who accuse Stanislavsky of neglecting the external elements of characterization. On the other hand, the book should serve as a form of catharsis for those bastardizers of Stanislavsky's theories whose chief concern is with their own emotional involvement rather than those of the character.[43]

While this battle was being fought, the Russian teachers who had toured with the MAT in the 1920s and were still alive downplayed the interior aspect of the System. At the same time, they seemed leery of directly criticizing

American interpretations, such as the Method, which did place great emphasis on emotions. For example, in the previously cited 1958 interview conducted by Arthur Gelb, Barbara Bulgakov spoke about the ability of Stanislavski's Method to release a talent and polish it by leading to a discovery and interpretation "of large truths, in a large theatrical way."[44] Bulgakov raged against small realities, such as buttoning a coat naturally, and actors who mumbled, techniques often associated with Strasberg's interpretation. Gelb stated that Bulgakov was distressed over the distortions of Stanislavski's approach that were currently circulating, although she had only the highest regard for Strasberg and believed that certain actors had misinterpreted some of his ideas. Tamara Daykarhanova actually belonged to the Actors Studio and performed the role of Anfisa, the nurse, in Strasberg's 1964 production of Anton Chekhov's *The Three Sisters*.[45]

ENTER SONIA MOORE

Contrary to the veiled disapproval from some Russians, Sonia Moore began her career in America by openly criticizing the Method and its proponents. Perhaps she believed that she had more to gain by setting the record straight about Stanislavski's work than by trying to fit into the theatre scene as it existed. It was a course of action that would put her at odds with most of those who wielded the power in American theatre.

Author Paul Gray makes no reference to Sonia Moore in his article on the chronology of the impact of Stanislavski's work in America. His article begins with the founding of the Moscow Art Theatre in 1897 and ends in "1964—and beyond" with the start of the repertory companies at Lincoln Center and the Actors Studio.[46] Christine Edwards, in her historically comprehensive 1965 text that sought to clarify the evolution of Stanislavski's technique in America, mentions Sonia Moore's 1957 letter to *New York Times* drama critic Brooks Atkinson in a note in the newspaper section of her bibliography, but not in the actual text.[47] By 1965 Moore had published her first textbook and was preparing for the revised version of it to come out. She had begun the Sonia Moore Studio of the Theatre and had directed Off-Broadway. However, the scope of Gray's and Edwards's works emphasized the historical evolution of Stanislavski's technique in America, and Moore's contribution apparently did not seem significant at that point.

One of the first acknowledgments of Sonia Moore as an expert on Stanislavski's work in theatrical literature was Erica Munk's 1966 text *Stanislavski and America*.[48] For this book, Munk had edited and reprinted an anthology of articles and interviews about Stanislavski from two special issues of *The Drama Review* (*TDR*), later issues of that journal, and unpublished sources. Moore's article, "The Method of Physical Actions," is in the

"Background" section of Munk's book.[49] It is a series of answers to questions sent to Moore by *TDR*. Moore's responses clarify the use of the Method of Physical Actions in training and rehearsals for every type of play, its link to Russian scientists, and how it relates to emotion and the subconscious.[50]

Moore's answers in Munk's text follow an edited selection of dialogue from a series of seminars held by representatives of the Moscow Art Theatre upon their visit to America in November and December 1964. This was the first MAT trip to the United States since their heralded tours in the 1920s.[51] In New York City, thirty to thirty-five practitioners of Stanislavski's technique in America were invited to the initial seminars.[52] One of the main topics of discussion was the current use of the Method of Physical Actions in the Soviet Union.

On December 13, 1964, Irving Drutman wrote an article about one of the seminars, entitled "Russian Method-ists Meet the American."[53] Drutman began the article by listing a number of well-known theatrical educators/artists in attendance at the lecture. Although he did not mention Sonia Moore, evidence indicates that she was present. He then proceeded to summarize what occurred as Vasily Toporkov, the Chair of Acting at the MAT, assured listeners that "the Russians were not there to teach, but only to share what they had learned first hand from Stanislavski."[54] According to Drutman, the Russians reminisced about Stanislavski's lessons, gave a boring explanation of some of his theory, and demonstrated parts of the System. This was followed by a question-and-answer session dominated by Shelley Winters talking about the use of emotional memory. Drutman wrote that Victor Manyukov, a prominent MAT director, concluded the sessions by stating that Stanislavski "attempted to base his method on emotion memory," and that he (Manyukov) could not "understand the confusion that existed in this country."[55]

Sonia Moore responded to Drutman's article on January 10, 1965. She openly contradicted Drutman's conclusion, writing that what Manyukov could not comprehend was why the Americans "limited themselves to discussing only Emotional Memory with which Stanislavski experimented in the 1920s."[56] Moore accused the Russians of failing "to convey that the Method of Physical Actions was the result of Stanislavski's life work and that because it is based on physiological law, it is the solution of an actor's problems of truthful emotions."[57] It appears that Moore was not only at the seminar, but she once again placed herself at the forefront of the controversy. She blamed the Russians for not emphasizing the Method of Physical Actions enough to clarify how wrong the Americans, such as actor Shelley Winters, were for focusing only on emotional memory.

Moore's attendance at this MAT symposium is corroborated by a letter from Vladimir Prokofieff, who at the time headed the Commission for Research of the Legacy of K. S. Stanislavski at the Moscow Art Theatre. Prokofieff was also one of the presenters at the Manhattan symposium. After the seminar, Moore sent Prokofieff the text of her lecture on Stanislavski's Method of Physical Actions. This was the basic lecture that she delivered at schools and other organizations around the country into the 1990s.

Prokofieff responded to Moore's lecture in July 1966. Although he noted that at that time her lecture served as a brief introduction, he commended her for presenting the main points of the Method of Physical Actions "concisely, concretely, and in a way accessible to all."[58] He praised her for striving to protect the System from "arbitrary primitivism." He also saluted her "activity directed toward the realization of Stanislavski's dream of the cultural and spiritual rapprochement of peoples of different countries on the road to the ideals of high art." Prokofieff urged Moore to stress the "interrelationship" of the physical and psychological more fervently and to include more about "the progressive philosophical and social purposefulness" of the whole System. He even offered to send her a copy of a new text that he was editing, written by Grigori V. Kristi, a close pupil of Stanislavski's. He claimed that the text was based "on the latest discoveries of Stanislavski about his method," and presented the full course of an actor's training according to the Stanislavski System, as practiced in the Soviet Union.[59]

Prokofieff's acknowledgment of Moore's comprehension of the Method of Physical Actions verifies that Moore was in line with Russian implementation of it. His suggestion that Moore stress "progressive philosophical and social purposefulness" seems to imply that Moore, at this early stage, did not incorporate enough of the Soviet point of view of the System in her writings and lectures. In assessing her entire body of work at a later date, theatre scholar Sharon M. Carnicke indicates that Moore's reliance on Russian information distorts the System because of what the Soviets edited out for political reasons.[60] For all her conscious reliance on Russian sources, however, Moore continued to search for ways to adapt Stanislavski's work, and not merely to imitate the Russians. She often asserted that even the Russians did not know what they were doing in the practice of the Stanislavski System!

The fact that Moore came out swinging rather than handshaking her way into the American theatre scene bruised some egos. Her independent, warrior-like attitude was perhaps her biggest asset, as well as her biggest liability; the Method of Physical Actions became her battle cry.

NOTES

1. Moscow Art Theatre instructor Inna Soloviova writes about the travails of Russian performers defecting to the United States. She explores in particular why Stanislavski may have chosen to return to Russia. See Inna Soloviova, "Do You Have Relatives Living Abroad? Emigration as a Cultural Problem," in *Wandering Stars: Rus-*

sian *Émigré Theatre, 1905–1940*, ed. Laurence Senelick (Iowa City: University of Iowa Press, 1992), 69–83.

2. Max Frankel, "Memories from Moscow," *New York Times*, sec. 2, October 26, 1958. See also, "Library in Tribute to Russian Actor," *New York Times*, sec. 1, November 2, 1958. In "Stage Art Exchange with Soviet Set Up," Arthur Gelb reported on "a large-scale exchange of original art work" to take place early in 1959. *New York Times*, sec. 1, November 17, 1958.

3. Harrison E. Salisbury, "Theatre Regains Its Vigor with New Faces and Ideas," *New York Times*, sec. 1, July 8, 1957.

4. Arthur Gelb, "Triumph of Nature over Method," *New York Times*, sec. 2, December 8, 1957.

5. Herbert Kupferberg, "The American Stanislavsky Theatre," draft copy, collection. of Philip G. Bennett.

6. Sonia Moore, "Letters Discuss Preston, the Method, Early Curtain and Other Topics," Drama Mailbag, *New York Times*, sec. 2, December 29, 1957.

7. Certainly, Stanislavsky's work and its derivatives are not the only acting-training techniques that exist. For an overall look at other techniques, see Phillip B. Zarrilli, ed., *Acting (Re)Considered*, 2nd ed. (New York: Routledge, 2002).

8. The Moscow Art Theatre gave a total of 380 performances in Manhattan, Brooklyn, Newark, New Haven, Hartford, Chicago, Boston, Cleveland, Detroit, Pittsburgh, and Washington, D.C. Sharon M. Carnicke, *Stanislavsky in Focus* (Amsterdam: Harwood Academic Publishers, 1998), 18.

9. Carnicke, *Stanislavsky in Focus*, 18.

10. Carnicke, *Stanislavsky in Focus*, 21.

11. Theatre scholar James H. McTeague challenges the popular notion that professional training in America owes its roots exclusively to Stanislavski. He details the theories and lessons of institutions in New York City and Boston, such as the oldest professional acting school in North America, the American Academy of Dramatic Arts, arguing that what he terms the "speculative" schools stressed acting theory and not merely the externalized, formulaic practices that dominated the commercial stage. He parallels similarities in the lessons taught in those schools with elements of Stanislavski's technique before it was known in this country. McTeague concludes that these schools are the real root of American acting training but that their alignment with the commercial theatre of the time allowed their techniques to be ignored in favor of Stanislavski's. James H. McTeague, *Before Stanislavsky: American Professional Acting Schools and Theory, 1875–1925* (Metuchen, N.J.: Scarecrow Press, 1993).

12. Carnicke has written one of the most recent accounts of the MAT's "legendary success" in America, describing how Stanislavski and his company were met with political ambiguity but artistic kudos. Carnicke, *Stanislavsky in Focus*, 13–33.

13. In fact, Boleslavsky first taught Stanislavski's technique in America before the inception of the American Lab Theatre, during the summer of 1923 at the Neighborhood Playhouse and in evening courses in the fall. Christine Edwards, *The Stanislavsky Heritage* (New York: New York University Press, 1965), 203, 240.

14. Literature about the Group Theatre is abundant. For example, director Harold Clurman's *The Fervent Years* (New York: Hill and Wang, 1957) is a good insider source. The December 1976 issue of the *Educational Theatre Journal* is

entitled "Reunion: A Self-Portrait of the Group Theatre" and is filled with photographs, a chronology, and personal memoirs of members' experiences. Also, Carnicke pulls together much of this historical information and analyzes the failures and successes of this icon of American theatre. Carnicke, *Stanislavsky in Focus*, 38–46.

15. Carnicke, *Stanislavsky in Focus*, 40.

16. It is well-known that Stella Adler met with Stanislavski in Paris for a short time while she belonged to the Group Theatre. When she returned to the Group, Adler's insistence that Stanislavski emphasized circumstances, imagination, and action caused a rift with Lee Strasberg, who maintained that emotional memory was the main element of the technique. Author Richard Brestoff points out that Adler herself did not like to use emotional memory insofar as it meant delving into her personal life, because she could find the emotions for a scene quite easily without it. Richard Brestoff, *The Great Acting Teachers and Their Methods* (Lyme, N.H.: Smith and Kraus, 1995), 118–19.

17. Additionally, of course, other acting legends, somewhat removed from the legacy of the Group Theatre but nevertheless espousing interpretations of Stanislavski's work, existed. For example, in 1947 director/actor Herbert Berghoff, one of the initial members of the Actors Studio, began the HB Studio. Berghoff, along with Uta Hagen, built the HB Studio on West Bank Street into a training ground for actors that still flourishes today. Hagen in particular, who died in 2003, was known as a brilliant teacher and actor. Her two texts, *Respect for Acting* (1973) and *A Challenge for the Actor* (1991), relate her own lengthy experience as an actor, offering valuable lessons to students on how she created characters through her Stanislavski-inspired work.

18. Charles Marowitz's recent biography of Chekhov is a comprehensive study of the artist. Marowitz, *The Other Chekhov: A Biography of Michael Chekhov, the Legendary Actor-Director and Theorist* (New York: Applause Books, 2004). For a chronology of Chekhov's life and accomplishments see Mel Gussow, "Michael Chekhov's Life and Work: A Chronology," *TDR* 27, no. 3 (1983): 1–21.

19. Chekhov is reputed, though, to have influenced a number of film actors, such as Jack Palance, Marilyn Monroe, and Anthony Quinn, all of whom he taught after he moved to Hollywood in 1943. Franc Chamberlain, "Michael Chekhov on the Technique of Acting," in *Twentieth Century Actor Training*, ed. Alison Hodge (New York: Routledge, 2000), 83–86.

20. Chekhov did write other texts and articles. See Lendley C. Black, *Michael Chekhov as Actor, Director and Teacher* (Ann Arbor: UMI Research Press, 1987), x–xii.

21. Franc Chamberlain claimed that it was also Deidre Hurst du Prey's transcription of Chekhov's *Lessons for the Professional Actor* in 1985, as well as the 1983 issue of *TDR* on Chekhov, that helped to renew interest in Chekhov's process. Mala Powers followed these works with a revision of *To the Actor* in 1991. A Chekhov International Workshop took place in the 1990s, too. Chamberlain, "Michael Chekhov on the Technique of Acting," 94–95.

22. As Paul Gray pointed out, however, none of the first generation of MAT actors, such as Olga Knipper, who developed their technique "unself-consciously" when the MAT began in 1898, directly affected the American theatre as teachers. Paul Gray,

"Stanislavski and America: A Critical Chronology," in "Stanislavski and America: 2," ed. Richard Schechner, special issue, *TDR* 9, no. 2 (Winter 1964): 25. See also Paul Gray, "A Critical Chronology," in *Stanislavski and America*, ed. Erica Munk (New York: Hill and Wang, 1966), 141. For a comprehensive look at the artistic practice of these First Studio but second-generation MAT members in America up until 1965, see Edwards, *Stanislavsky Heritage*, 241–45.

23. Although Andrius Jilinsky died in 1948, his thoughts on acting were not published until 1989. Jilinsky, *The Joy of Acting: A Primer for Actors*, ed. Helen C. Bragdon (New York: Peter Lang, 1989). For a personal account of Jilinsky and his teaching, see Mary Hunter Wolf, "Reminiscences of Andrius Jilinsky and His Teaching," in Senelick, *Wandering Stars*, 129–39.

24. After teaching at the American Lab Theatre, Maria Ouspenskaya taught at the Neighborhood Playhouse until she opened her own studio in 1931. In 1936 she went out to Hollywood for a film career and opened a studio in Los Angeles, teaching and performing until her death in 1949. Edwards, *Stanislavsky Heritage*, 241.

25. Brochure, *Tamara Daykarhanova School for the Stage*, n.d., Tamara Daykarhanova Papers, New York Public Library for the Performing Arts.

26. Edwards, *Stanislavsky Heritage*, 241.

27. "L. Bulgakov Dead; Leader in Theatre," *New York Times*, July 21, 1948, nytimes.com (accessed June 10, 2003).

28. Gray, "A Critical Chronology," 41.

29. Hunter Wolf, "Reminiscences of Andrius Jilinsky," 130. A telegram to Oliver Sayler, the American representative for the Moscow Art Theatre, states that Stanislavski and Nemirovich-Danchenko wanted the press to know that the Moscow Art Players were not connected to the MAT, except for the fact that some of the Moscow Art Players had been with the MAT at one time. Konstantin Stanislavski and Vladimir Nemirovich-Danchenko to Oliver Sayler, Moscow Art Players Papers, New York Public Library for the Performing Arts.

30. The Habima Theatre was begun in Russia in 1918 by Alexander Granovsky and was composed of Jewish actors. It toured extensively, eventually settling in Israel and becoming Israel's national theatre. Oscar G. Brockett and Robert Findlay, *Century of Innovation*, 2nd ed. (Boston: Allyn and Bacon, 1991), 189.

31. Arthur Gelb, "Two and Two Are Five," *New York Times*, sec. 2, February 2, 1958.

32. Both Tamiroff and Baclanova eventually went to Hollywood after arriving in America with the Moscow Art Theatre. Tamiroff taught at Daykarhanova's Stage Make-up School, and was active with the Theatre Guild before going west in the 1930s. He made over forty-five movies. Baclanova played on Broadway before her first big film role in *Street of Sin* in 1928. Her most famous movie was the horror classic *Freaks*. No evidence suggests that she taught.

33. Gray, "A Critical Chronology," 40–41.

34. Gray, "A Critical Chronology," 40.

35. A look at the acting studios that existed in New York City from the late 1950s to the early 1960s reveals that besides the schools still run by Daykarhanova and Soloviova, and the ones that had existed since the 1920s, such as the American Academy of Dramatic Arts, the Neighborhood Playhouse, and the American Theatre Wing, there were the Stella Adler Theatre Studio, the HB Studio, and a number of lesser-known ones.

Among the latter were Jack Manning's Shakespeare Lab, Players Workshop with Norma Hayes and Jutta Wolf, Actors Mobile Theatre, Manhattan Theatre Arts Center, Eli Rill Theatre Workshop, Theatre Studio of New York, and the Anthony Manning Studio. Individual acting coaches also were numerous.

36. For Strasberg's own explanation of his process at the Actors Studio see, for example, Richard Schechner, "Working with Live Material: An Interview with Lee Strasberg," in Munk, *Stanislavski and America*, 183–200. Also, for remarks from famous actors, anonymous students, and a psychiatrist about the psychological impact of Strasberg's training, see Gray, "Stanislavski and America: A Critical Chronology," 47–52.

37. Edwards, *Stanislavsky Heritage*, 261.

38. Seymour Peck, "The Temple of the 'Method,'" *New York Times Magazine*, May 6, 1956, 26–27, 42, 47–48.

39. Jack Gould, "Exclusive Folks: Introspective TV Actors Make Viewers Feel as if They're Rude Interlopers," *New York Times*, May 27, 1956, nytimes.com (accessed December 12, 2004).

40. Drama Mailbag, *New York Times*, June 3, 1956.

41. Lee Strasberg, "View from The Studio," *New York Times*, September 2, 1956.

42. Drama Mailbag, *New York Times*, September 16, 1956.

43. Edwards, *Stanislavsky Heritage*, 264.

44. Gelb, "Two and Two Are Five," 1.

45. As Edwards pointed out in her text, the September 1964 issue of *TDR* offered a revealing comparison of answers from Soloviova, Adler, and Meisner in one article, and from Strasberg in another, as to the differences between the Method and Stanislavski's System. Edwards, *Stanislavsky Heritage*, 269–73.

46. Gray, "A Critical Chronology," 58.

47. Edwards, *Stanislavsky Heritage*, 324.

48. By this time, Moore had been recognized as an expert elsewhere, for example, in newspapers through interviews and articles.

49. Sonia Moore, "The Method of Physical Actions," in *Stanislavski and America*, 73–76.

50. In that same text, an article by scholar Leslie Irene Coger used Moore's assertion that Stanislavski rejected his initial belief of evoking emotion in favor of finding a way for the actor to summon up "the necessary unconscious experience" through physical action. Through it, Coger bolstered her own argument about Stanislavski's change in methodology. Coger, "Stanislavski Changes His Mind," in Munk, *Stanislavski and America*, 60–65.

51. The MAT visitors also conducted seminars in New Haven, New Orleans, and Ann Arbor. Munk pointed out that the remarks in her text were from a tape made in New Orleans. "Stanislavski Preserved: An MAT Discussion," in *Stanislavski and America*, 66–73. Stella Adler is credited with suggesting that the conference take place. Edwards, *Stanislavsky Heritage*, 281–82.

52. After the initial series of seminars for the theatrical figureheads in New York, two larger sessions were offered for Equity members and for specially invited students. Edwards, *Stanislavsky Heritage*, 282.

53. Irving Drutman, "Russian Method-ists Meet the American," *New York Times*, December 13, 1964, nytimes.com (accessed July 10, 2003).

54. Drutman, "Russian Method-ists Meet the American."

55. Drutman, "Russian Method-ists Meet the American."

56. Sonia Moore, "Views from the Drama Mailbag," *New York Times*, January 10, 1965, nytimes.com (accessed July 10, 2003).

57. Moore, "Views from the Drama Mailbag."

58. Vladimir Prokofieff to Sonia Moore, July 1966, Sonia Moore Papers, New York Public Library for the Performing Arts.

59. Part of this text by Kristi is included in a collection of excerpts from other Russian experts on Stanislavski that Sonia Moore translated and published in 1973. Grigori V. Kristi, "The Training of an Actor in the Stanislavski School of Acting," in *Stanislavski Today*, trans. and ed. Sonia Moore (New York: American Center for Stanislavski Theatre Art, 1973), 22–33.

60. Carnicke, *Stanislavsky in Focus*, 214.

3

The Method of Physical Actions: A Russian [R]Evolution

In order to appreciate Sonia Moore's commitment to the Method of Physical Actions, it helps to understand the evolution of Stanislavski's quest for stage truth. As a young actor and director Stanislavski was acutely aware of the state of Russian theatre in the early part of the twentieth century. Much of what he witnessed and experienced on stage was uninspiring. His search for inspiration on stage drove him to study the work of great actors and to seek out people, theories, and ideas in an effort to acquire new knowledge or to reformulate old notions. He spent forty years researching, developing, and refining a system of acting that would enable any actor to achieve consistently what the gifted performer could attain effortlessly. Stanislavski conceived a grammar of stage art "because his method is to theatre what grammar is to literature. Grammar enables you to write correctly. But what you write, that's another matter. . . . A thousand years will pass . . . but the laws of human behavior that Stanislavski discovered are eternal."[1]

THE CREATION OF THE SYSTEM

By the time of his famous meeting with Vladimir Nemirovich-Danchenko in 1897 that resulted in the founding of the Moscow Art Theatre, Stanislavski was already struggling with the artistic issues that would keep him occupied for the rest of his life. Pursuing the solution to spontaneity on stage began with his critical analysis of his own performance as well as his study of other performers. Through observation of brilliant actors he was able to isolate and record and test the elements of what he considered to be stage truth. He eventually developed a technique designed to train the actors of the Moscow

Art Theatre, since no systematized approach to the actor's work existed at that time. Inspiration on the stage might be achieved unconsciously, but there were no guarantees that it could be repeated at future performances.

Early in the development of his System, Stanislavski believed that a variety of elements—relaxation, concentration, belief, imagination, and emotional memory, among others—were responsible for the actor's creative state. Though Stanislavski never rejected the part that each of these elements plays in the overall process of invention, it became clear that any one of them alone was not sufficient to generate stage truth. They became means to ends, rather than ends in themselves.

Stanislavski focused his restless intellect on philosophical and scientific literature to support an experimental approach to the formulation of his grammar of acting. He was fascinated with scientific research and curious regarding contemporary discoveries in behavioral psychology. The study of human behavior would intersect naturally with his interests and growing realizations regarding the psychology of the performance process. One of the first scientists he studied was French psychologist Théodule Ribot, whose theories on affective memory became the basis for Stanislavski's work on emotional memory. Ribot's books were translated into Russian, and Stanislavski owned six of them.[2]

He was particularly interested in Ribot's assertion that the nervous system records memories of past emotions, which may be evoked by appropriate stimuli. "A touch, a sound, a smell may enable [one] to relive not just one experience but a grouping of similar experiences which merge to create a single emotional state."[3] Though Ribot made a distinction between *concrete* memories of emotion, which are felt as strongly as original emotions, and *abstract* memories of feelings, which are intellectual and substitutes for the real thing, he noted that emotion memory was a rare experience and "nil in the majority of people."[4] Nevertheless, Stanislavski grabbed hold of Ribot's theories and found them a useful way to study the psychological life of a character. Ribot viewed emotion as a unified, psychophysical event "with no causal relationship between mind and body." The "indissoluble link between mind and body" that he articulated provided a scientific basis for Stanislavski's artistic discoveries.[5]

By the time the System began to emerge during rehearsal for Stanislavski's production of *Hamlet* in 1909, changes from previous MAT performances were already under way. For example, the detailed preproduction plan was eliminated.

> Production values were not the main concern. The process of creating the performance depended on delicate collaborative work with the actor. For the first time Stanislavski's production book shows the action broken down into sections or "units." The rehearsal process consisted in finding the feelings, the psychological states, contained in those sections and in relating them, through emotion memory, to personal experience.[6]

At this point, as the focus was psychological, emotional memory was the centerpiece of the System. Once emotional states were discovered intuitively with the director's guidance, physical action was used merely to "illustrate and fix the emotional states."[7] Yet, Stanislavski was aware of the limitations of depending on emotional memory to stir the actor's feelings. By having the actor relive his own storehouse of emotional experiences he encouraged a personal involvement with the character. But, often, the result for the actor was negative: self-indulgence, tension, exhaustion, and, sometimes, hysteria. The actor ran the risk of losing himself in personal emotion and therefore losing contact with the role. (Eventually, Stanislavski acknowledged that it is more difficult for the actor to define what he *feels* than what he *does* in exactly the same set of circumstances.)[8]

THE PSYCHOPHYSICAL CONNECTION

Other scientists provided material that also fueled Stanislavski's imagination. Ivan Sechenov's and Ivan Pavlov's work on reflexes and conditioning provided a basis for the notion of psychophysical unity. In his research, Sechenov clarified the importance of "reflex" as the primary means of organic response, while Pavlov viewed the "reflex" as the "central phenomenon of psychic life."[9] Though scholars are uncertain whether or not Stanislavski had actual contact with Pavlov, their individual discoveries and interests coincided.[10] His experiments with physical action reflected Pavlov's work with conditioned reflexes and resulted in a similar conclusion: "The mind and body are so intimately connected that they stimulate and influence each other. Every mental process . . . is immediately transmitted through the body in visual expression. Human behavior . . . becomes a continuous, uninterrupted psychophysical process."[11]

As Stanislavski absorbed the "implications of contemporary psychophysiological theory" he made adjustments to his System to account for emerging information. Theatre scholar Joseph R. Roach suggests that "his System cannot be comprehended without his science."[12] By presenting the notion of an unbreakable bond between a personal experience and its objective expression, Stanislavski demonstrated that it was possible to create the emotional life of a role by reaching the subconscious through conscious means. He did not, however, diminish the importance of the actor's emotional memory. He knew that emotions were delicate things that needed to be coaxed out of hiding, evoked not directly, but indirectly. Stanislavski's search for an effective way to tap into the inner life of the role shifted from the "subjective world of memory and emotion" to the "concrete physical world of actions and events."[13]

As early as 1916 the term *physical action* appeared in rehearsal commentary and in correspondence between Stanislavski and his coworkers. In that year he delivered a series of lectures that demonstrated a revision in his thinking. Referring to the actor's work on a role, he advised, "'Put yourself in the circumstances of the character as portrayed and put the questions: what would I do in such a circumstance, what do I want. . . . Answer them with verbs which express actions.'"[14] Here, Stanislavski does not suggest premeditated use of emotional memory. The actor's personal history becomes involved unconsciously. This is the seed of the System in its final form, the Method of Physical Actions.[15]

Writing in 1924, Stanislavski summed up his recognition of the connection between the psychological and the physical: "In each physical act there is an inner psychological motive which impels physical action, as in every psychological inner action there is also physical action, which expresses its psychic nature. *The union of these two actions results in organic action on the stage.*"[16] He never abandoned the psychological in favor of the physical; he simply intended to move forward into new areas of exploration, giving his System greater concreteness. An incident during the rehearsal of *Tartuffe* (1936–1938), described by one of the company members, points this out:

> At that time he considered the foundation of his system to be the work on physical actions, and he brushed away all that might distract the actors from its significance. When we reminded him of his much earlier methods, he naively pretended that he didn't understand what we were talking about. Once someone asked:
> "What is the nature of the 'emotional states' of the actors in this scene?"
> Konstantin Sergeyevich looked surprised and said:
> "'Emotional states?' What is that? I never heard of it."
> That was not true. At one time this expression had been used by Stanislavski himself. Nevertheless, in this case he kept us from fixing our attention on it and directed us to the desired channel. He was afraid of all backward glances which could interfere with reaching his goal.[17]

The issue of Stanislavski's alteration and development of his System has generated substantial discussion. Some scholars have attributed his change of mind to the process of examination and discovery. Moore considered his early experiments failures, and in her opinion he did not find the answer to his forty-year quest until, aided by science, he crafted the Method of Physical Actions. Carnicke has indicated that his shift to the physical side of the creative process was the result of Soviet politics and that the concrete reality of the Method of Physical Actions meshed more closely with the Soviet philosophy of Socialist Realism.[18] Regardless of the reasons, and most probably there were several, by 1931 Stanislavski relegated the "'work on oneself' and 'the work on one's role,' which he had pioneered from 1909 to 1931 . . . to the classroom studio" and focused his attention on physical action in rehearsal.[19]

THE EMERGENCE OF THE
METHOD OF PHYSICAL ACTIONS

Stanislavski established two patterns throughout his career whenever he wished to study acting technique. One was to take a laboratory approach to his research. In the beginning, he served as his own laboratory and explored his acting and directing during rehearsals of productions at the Moscow Art Theatre. This was a routine that continued to the end of his life and that often resulted in a time lag between his personal practice as recorded in his notes and the public presentation of the System. This discrepancy between what he said and what he did produced criticism, even from close colleagues and students.[20] In 1912, by which time Stanislavski had identified the primary elements of his System and was beginning to shape them into a coherent whole, he felt the need to broaden his research. As a result, he founded the First Studio of the Moscow Art Theatre to explore the System and put it into practice.

The second pattern of exploration that Stanislavski established early on concerned the type of laboratory he created. When the First Studio was formed, Stanislavski's unsuccessful attempts to experiment with veteran actors of the MAT convinced him that he needed to work with fresh, relatively inexperienced, but talented, young artists. The acting company of the First Studio included such future luminaries as Michael Chekhov, Richard Boleslavsky, and Evgeni Vakhtangov. The acting process at this point was based on the use of emotional memory. In the years that followed he continued this process of seeking out young actors who were not completely fixed in their ways of thinking and acting. He helped to launch, or participated in, the Second Studio and Vakhtangov's Drama Studio, later to become the Third Studio, in addition to less well-known studios.

So it is not surprising that, in keeping with this spirit of renewal, in 1935 Stanislavski called together a group of actors and directors in an effort to undertake his final research, and formed the Opera-Dramatic Studio. He made it clear that the work was not focused on performance but was instead an exploration: he believed that all great actors needed to revitalize their art every four or five years by reentering "school."[21] While rehearsing *Hamlet, Romeo and Juliet, The Cherry Orchard*, and *Tartuffe*, Stanislavski created what came to be known as the Method of Physical Actions or the "method of analysis through physical action."[22] He now rehearsed according to a simple truth: by establishing a line of logical physical actions that reveal character truthfully the internal life of the character unfolds naturally.

From 1935 onward, actors were urged to keep within the confines of physical actions. They began with simple objectives, moved on to form the physical life of the role, and from there moved forward to shape the spiritual life of the role. With the Method of Physical Actions, Stanislavski replaced the long period around the table dissecting the play with a brief discussion of the superobjective and major events, followed by an analysis of the play through improvisations on actions. Through structured improvisations, "the actor defines his role as a sequence of psychophysical objectives and events. As he builds the character . . . he consciously constructs a chain of stimulating actions. . . . When he has fixed the sequence or score through many repetitions, spontaneity returns."[23]

Though Stanislavski did not record a detailed description of his work, he did provide summaries from time to time. Shortly before his death in June 1938, he presented an outline, broken down into three stages, for working on a play. During the first stage, the director established the superobjective of the play and identified large episodes and smaller incidents, determining basic actions for each character in each incident. Through discussion, the director and actors then identified the series of events that constructed the plot, and actors established their individual sequences of physical actions. In the second phase, the text was analyzed to establish a logical succession of ideas and images and to determine the sequence of objectives. Actors improvised the text with random words or phrases. Finally, in the third stage, the director and actors meshed the defined lines of physical actions with the images and inner monologues generated by the actors. Simultaneously, the actors performed exercises and improvisations to deepen their work and to "fill out the gaps in the script."[24]

Further rehearsal time was devoted to a more detailed study of the episodes and incidents in the play and investigation of the given circumstances, particularly with regard to period manners and behavior. Gradually actors established the inner and outer characteristics of the role and fixed the specific tempo-rhythm for each incident, episode, and character and for the play as a whole. The goal was precise physical actions leading to precise emotions communicated by precise vocal and physical expression.[25] Though this was the last commentary that Stanislavski offered on his new Method, it is probable that he did not consider it definitive and would have continued to refine the working process had he lived.[26]

Fragments of notes from rehearsals during this period are included in *Creating a Role*, the last of his books on the System, which was published in America in 1961. Members of his acting company also left accounts of rehearsals, such as *Stanislavski in Rehearsal* by Vasily Toporkov. Because so little was written down, information about the Method of Physical Actions depended on the oral tradition developed by his last students—for example, Toporkov, Mikhail Kedrov, and Maria Knebel, who were working with him at the time of his death and passed this "lore about action" on to their own students.[27]

In *Stanislavski in Rehearsal* Toporkov provides both personal and professional insights into the Method of Physical Actions in practice. Stanislavski's intentions were clear from the beginning. The pursuit of a logical, consecutive line of physical actions is not simply the pursuit of physical movement; it is the pursuit of psychophysical action, which includes the psychological task. "'There is no physical action without volition, without objectives and problems, and without inner justification of them by one's feelings.'"[28] Stanislavski was equally clear about the place of emotion in the rehearsal process: "'If your feelings dry up, there is no cause for alarm; simply return to physical actions and these will restore your lost feelings. . . . We cannot remember feelings and fix them. . . . We can just remember the line of physical actions.'"[29]

From Toporkov's perspective, analyzing the script and characters via the Method of Physical Actions was sometimes like "entertaining play." Improvisations were used to explore the behavior of characters until the appropriate physical actions were found to support the given task or until improvisations "reached a point where they demanded greater expressiveness through the author's words."[30] Logic and the consistency of the character's behavior were repeatedly reinforced. Stanislavski warned his actors that if he did not believe the logic of their actions, they would not be able to convince him of anything.

REHEARSAL PRACTICE

The Method of Physical Actions, as Stanislavski had developed it by the end of his life, required painstaking attention to detail, to the individual events, episodes, tasks, and, ultimately, physical actions that created a score of behavior for the character, which demanded an enormous commitment of time and effort. By Stanislavski's death the company had rehearsed *Tartuffe* for two years and had yet to run through a whole act. At some point a few years before 1938, Stanislavski enumerated the steps involved in the use of the Method of Physical Actions. This twenty-five-point plan summarizes the day-to-day activity of the director and actors, and in a simplified form it includes the following:

1. Before reading the play with the actors, the director explains the plot.
2. Using the given circumstances, the actors improvise the actions of the play.
3. Through improvisation, the actors explore the past and future of the characters.
4. The director tells the story in greater detail, producing more circumstances and "Magic Ifs," asking what would actors do "if" they found themselves in the characters' positions.
5. The director outlines the play's superobjective.

6. The actors create their characters' primary actions.
7. The play is broken down into large physical units and actions.
8. Using the "Magic If," actors perform the physical actions.
9. Actors break the physical actions into smaller segments, paying attention to the logic and continuity of the larger units.
10. The director and actors establish the logic and believability of the actions through repetition.
11. The logic and believability of events are set so that actors feel they could happen in the present.
12. Through improvisation, actors create an active state of "I am" as if the event is happening right here and now.
13. Through improvisation, the actors absorb their characters' psychology into their own subconscious.
14. The actors read the play for the first time.
15. Using the given circumstances, the actors study the text and justify their actions.
16. The actors improvise the play, replacing dialogue with nonsense syllables.
17. Actors set the text in the context of justified actions. While still speaking nonsense syllables, they verbalize inner monologues and share these with scene partners.
18. Around the table, actors read the play to each other and suggest their physical actions.
19. Actors read the play again using only their head and hands to demonstrate physical activity.
20. Actors read their parts on stage using rough blocking.
21. Actors discuss their ideas for the stage setting.
22. Actors are introduced to the actual setting and explore possible locations for their actions.
23. Actors experiment with the staging by opening up each of the four walls.
24. Actors discuss the meaning of the play from sociopolitical and artistic perspectives.
25. The director provides external characterization for actors who need assistance in this area.[31]

THE CONFUSION

Though the roots of the Method of Physical Actions are found throughout the four decades of Stanislavski's career, his earlier discoveries were firmly established in the minds of many theatre artists, especially in America. Without his writing down the Method of Physical Actions in some detail, there would, understandably, be a problem with the theatre world accepting this rehearsal process as a cornerstone of the Stanislavski System. It has been suggested that as a system of actor training, the Method of Physical Actions is limited by the skill of those teaching it.[32] In a 1933 letter to Maxim Gorky, when he was already experimenting with physical action, Stanislavski acknowledged some of his frustration with the perceptions of his work:

> I have harnessed my mind to the task of putting on paper, as concisely and clearly as I can, what a beginning actor should know. Such a book is needed if only to put an end to all of the twisted interpretations put on my so-called "system" which, in the way it is presently being taught, can put young actors on quite the wrong path.[33]

Contributing to the confusion regarding Stanislavski's System and the relationship between the psychological and physical aspects of the actor's work was the fact that *An Actor Prepares* (1936) and *Building a Character* (1949) were translated, edited, and published separately, over ten years apart, in the United States. In the Russian version, they were actually Parts I and II of the same work: *An Actor's Work on Himself.* Stanislavski's intention was to link the psychological (*An Actor Prepares*) and the physical (*Building a Character*) more closely theoretically and practically.

Recognizing the conflicts raised by the introduction of Stanislavski's new Method, Toporkov remarks that "some of our leading theatre workers and critics have branded Stanislavski's technique mere 'mathematics' or 'mechanics.' This has come about because the new technique has been mastered by very few and is not perfectly clear to others. Learning it presents great difficulties."[34] Indeed, Stanislavski's new Method required of the director "vigilance, persistence, the ability to interest the actors and to awaken their imagination." On the other hand, actors now had "material for the most complete development of all the features of the character."[35]

When Stanislavski gathered together the cast of *Tartuffe* he was testing and summarizing not only his new working method but the laws of human nature that he had discovered as he experimented with the creative process. His lifelong search for artistic truth ended with his death in 1938. He had, however, by this point begun to articulate a technique to help the actor tap into sources of inspiration, to provide expressive control over a living organism.[36] Maria Knebel, one of his last disciples, reflected on her realization of his achievement:

> When I first became acquainted with this new method in 1935 . . . I thought Stanislavski had eliminated everything that he himself had known and established. Then, as the years passed, I came to understand. . . . The new method absorbs everything discovered by him before. . . . Without understanding this, one cannot grasp the novelty of the discovery. The fact of the discovery cannot fail to stun us even today.[37]

NOTES

1. Alma Law, "An 'Actor's Director' Debuts in the West: A Conversation with Russia's Georgi Tovstonogov," *American Theatre* (June 1987): 19, 45.
2. Sharon M. Carnicke, *Stanislavsky in Focus* (Amsterdam: Harwood Academic Publishers, 1998), 131–32.
3. Jean Benedetti, *Stanislavski: A Biography* (New York: Routledge, 1988), 175.
4. Carnicke, *Stanislavsky in Focus*, 132–33.
5. Carnicke, *Stanislavsky in Focus*, 139.
6. Benedetti, *Stanislavski: A Biography*, 180.
7. Benedetti, *Stanislavski: A Biography*, 187–88.
8. Constantin Stanislavski, *Stanislavski's Legacy*, ed. and trans. Elizabeth Reynolds Hapgood (New York: Theatre Arts Books, 1958), 47.
9. Joseph R. Roach, *The Player's Passion* (Newark: University of Delaware Press, 1985), 198, 206.
10. P. V. Simonov, "The Method of K. S. Stanislavski and the Physiology of Emotion," in *Stanislavski Today*, trans. and ed. Sonia Moore (New York: American Center for Stanislavski Theatre Art, 1973), 37. Russian neurophysiologist Simonov indicates that there was contact between Stanislavski and Pavlov. Sonia Moore initially reinforces this idea (*Stanislavski System*, 1965) but later suggests that it is not known if they actually met (*Stanislavski System*, 1984).
11. Sonia Moore, *Stanislavski Revealed: The Solution to Spontaneity on Stage* (New York: Applause Theatre Book Publishers, 1991), 5–6.
12. Roach, *Player's Passion*, 20.
13. Roach, *Player's Passion*, 211.
14. Benedetti, *Stanislavski*, 217. The author quotes Stanislavski from the K. S. Archive No. 1388/1.
15. Benedetti, *Stanislavski*, 217.
16. Stanislavski, *Stanislavski's Legacy*, 11–12.
17. Vasily Toporkov, *Stanislavski in Rehearsal*, trans. Christine Edwards (New York: Theatre Arts Books, 1979), 157.
18. Carnicke, *Stanislavsky in Focus*, 150, 167.
19. Mel Gordon, *The Stanislavsky Technique* (New York: Applause Theatre Book Publishers, 1987), 207.
20. Benedetti, *Stanislavski*, 200. Benedetti indicates that some of the sharpest criticism came from Vakhtangov, who felt that the discrepancy suggested that Stanislavski was "betraying his own ideals."
21. Toporkov, *Stanislavski in Rehearsal*, 155.
22. Benedetti, *Stanislavski*, 315–16.
23. Roach, *Player's Passion*, 213.
24. Benedetti, *Stanislavski*, 316–17.
25. Benedetti, *Stanislavski*, 317–18.
26. Benedetti, *Stanislavski*, 317. The author suggests that in 1936 Stanislavski was torn between the necessity to honor his book contract for the publication of *An Actor Prepares*, which focused on his earlier work from 1908 to 1914, and his desire to include his new ideas on the Method of Physical Actions (315). No sooner had *An*

Actor Prepares appeared in America than Stanislavski was revising it and drafting new material.

27. Carnicke, *Stanislavsky in Focus*, 153.

28. Toporkov, *Stanislavski in Rehearsal*, 16.

29. Toporkov, *Stanislavski in Rehearsal*, 162, 173.

30. Toporkov, *Stanislavski in Rehearsal*, 87, 177.

31. What is included here is an abbreviated form of the twenty-five steps listed in Gordon, 209–12. This rehearsal plan is also included in Appendix A of Stanislavski's book *Creating a Role* in a longer and somewhat convoluted form. Constantin Stanislavski, *Creating a Role*, ed. Elizabeth Reynolds Hapgood, trans. Hermione I. Popper (New York: Theatre Arts Books, 1961), 253–55.

32. Gordon, *Stanislavsky Technique*, 212.

33. Stanislavski, *Stanislavski's Legacy*, 206.

34. Toporkov, *Stanislavski in Rehearsal*, 217.

35. Toporkov, *Stanislavski in Rehearsal*, 165.

36. Roach, *Player's Passion*, 206.

37. M. O. Knebel, "The Nemirovitch-Dantchenko School of Directing," in Moore, *Stanislavski Today*, 45.

4

Sonia Moore's Books: Interpreting the Stanislavski System for American Actors

Once Sonia Moore received encouragement to write her first book, there was no turning back. Three years after her letter to the *New York Times*, she published *The Stanislavski Method* (1960), later revised as the *Stanislavski System* (1965, 1974, 1984), followed by two editions of *Training an Actor* (1968, 1979), and concluding with *Stanislavski Revealed* (1991). In 1973 she also translated and edited a series of articles on Stanislavski and his System titled *Stanislavski Today*. In the course of her career Sonia Moore used her books as a forum to communicate her growing body of research on Stanislavksi and various aspects of his System. Her evolution as a theatre artist is clearly reflected in her writing, and her books have become her most lasting, and arguably most important, legacy to the theatre. The content of these texts provides an overview of her developing perspective on Stanislavski, acting technique, American theatre, and, finally, the Method of Physical Actions.

In an interview with Sonia Moore in September 1988 Michael Fitzsousa indicates that the book she "accidentally" discovered on her trip to England in 1957 was *An Actor Prepares*.[1] However, it seems doubtful that she was greatly influenced by Stanislavski's first book since, in a letter to the editor of *The Drama Review* in 1973, Moore dismissed *An Actor Prepares* because it contained Stanislavski's "obsolete deductions."[2]

By 1957 both *An Actor Prepares* and *Building a Character* had been published in the United States, but neither book referred to the Method of Physical Actions. *Creating a Role*, which did discuss the Method of Physical Actions, was not published until 1961. Published books by and about Stanislavski available in English in 1957 included *Stanislavsky on the Art of the Stage*, which was translated by David Magarshack (1950), and *Stanislavsky Directs* by N. M. Gorchakov (1954), among others. Both authors describe Stanislavski's System in theory and in practice and refer clearly to his improvisational working method that concentrated on physical action. In the introduction to *Stanislavski on the Art of the Stage*, Magarshack reiterates Stanislavski's advice to the actor to "leave the complex psychological problem alone" and "transfer his attention to . . . the logic of actions."[3]

Nearly all of Sonia Moore's resource materials in the 1950s and 1960s were Russian books and articles that had not been translated and therefore would have been unfamiliar to most American theatre artists. But her dependence on Russian sources was complicated. Following Stanislavski's death, his students and colleagues scrambled to communicate their own perceptions of his legacy, resulting in disagreements regarding his intentions and final results.[4] Committees were established to study him, books were written to explain him, and a series of scholars debated his contribution. In *Stanislavski Today*, Moore translated essays by a variety of Stanislavski's disciples, including Maria Knebel, Grigori Kristi, Georgi Tovstonogov, and Boris Zakhava, as well as by Soviet neurophysiologist P. V. Simonov. This compilation demonstrates the degree to which she was influenced by Soviet material.

Some Russian authorities, however, might have been guilty of expressing a Soviet bias in their writing: "By privileging the body over the psyche, by relying on behaviourist theories, and by regarding even the actor's work on a play as 'a dialectical process of analysis and synthesis,'" Soviet interpreters of Stanislavksi were making his "career palatable to Marxist materialism."[5] Sonia Moore has been faulted for accepting Soviet opinion, and scientist P. V. Simonov's views in particular, as "unquestionably reliable." After all, some Russian scientists and theatre artists "had made it their jobs to adjust Stanislavsky to the powers that be."[6] This "adjustment" of Stanislavski is reinforced, for example, in an article published in 1971 by Simonov. In it he comments on Stanislavski's encouraging actors to send out "rays" from their eyes as a means of creating communion with fellow actors. Simonov insists that the term *rays* creates "an impression of vexing dissonance. It is outwardly in clear contradiction with the materialistic principles of the System." To avoid any notion of mysticism, he explains that *rays* refer to "micromimics, tiny movements of expression, especially convulsions of mimic muscles, which cause the so-called expression of the eyes. . . . No 'rays' exist, of course."[7]

Questions remain regarding Soviet interpretation of the Method of Physical Actions, its practicality in rehearsal, and its relationship to the whole of the System. Some American theatre scholars would disagree with Sonia Moore that it was Stanislavski's final and most important legacy. While there is no doubt that Russian influences permeated her research, her efforts to promote Stanislavski resulted in her studying the System in depth. By analyzing the content of her books and comparing initial publications with subsequent revisions, it is possible to trace her growing understanding of the Method of Physical Actions.

THE STANISLAVSKI METHOD (1960)

The Stanislavski Method was written to correct misconceptions and clarify Stanislavski's work in order to create a straightforward acting text for American actors. The use of "Method" in her title might have been intended to separate "Stanislavski's" method from the "American" method with which it has often been confused. In her introduction she acknowledged that the Stanislavski method was mired in problems from the beginning. Initially perceived as convoluted and uninteresting by prominent Russian actors (5),[8] the System was not accepted by some of the great artists whose work formed the basis of the technique. Stanislavski himself indicated that he was overwhelmed by the enormous quantity of material he had amassed. Moore concluded that the manner in which it was presented in his own books was too difficult to understand, and so she chose to simplify his theories to make them more accessible (6).

By all accounts she was highly successful. Reviews of *The Stanislavski Method* indicated that her book was a "brief, lucid, and sensible explanation of . . . Stanislavski" and the "first simplified guide to the widely publicized but much misunderstood Method." One reviewer suggested that "she gives the clearest and most concise—and perhaps the most easily assimilated—account of the master's method . . . yet encountered."[9]

Sonia Moore felt, from the beginning, that the lack of Russian material translated into English contributed to a misunderstanding of Stanislavski's work in the United States. The sources noted in the bibliography of *The Stanislavski Method* are Russian books dating from the 1920s to the late 1950s, including the six volumes of the *Complete Works of Stanislavski* published from 1954 through 1959. The texts range from Stanislavski's *My Life in Art* and several books by N. M. Gorchakov to works about Vakhtangov and other prominent Russian artists. Two of the books were published by the Academy of Science of the USSR.

Moore asserts that Stanislavski's writing was not meant to be read and discussed, but to be studied and practiced. She felt that few actors realized that Stanislavski considered acting technique to be a meshing of the psychological and the physical, a joining of the inner experience with its outer expression. Stanislavski, according to Moore, taught actors that the rehearsal period was a search for action, not for lengthy discussions (9). Her insistence that Stanislavski's System was not a doctrine to be followed slavishly but a living, growing process echoed his own attitude about his work and supported her contention that if Stanislavski were alive today he would still be refining his System.

Key chapters in *The Stanislavski Method* demonstrate Moore's recognition of his focus on physical action. For example, in chapter 3, "The Method," she begins the discussion of the elements of the System with a section titled "Action, 'If,' Given Circumstances." Immediately, she clarifies her point of view: Stanislavski's Method is about action—purposeful, logical, inner, and external action. Emotional memory is not discussed until much later in the chapter. Though the word *psychophysical* does not appear in *The Stanislavski Method*, she assumes it when she says physical actions have a psychological meaning. Truthful emotions will emerge spontaneously when prompted by simple physical actions that grow out of given circumstances (42).

Sonia Moore initiates a pattern of distancing herself from adherents of the American Method when she writes about emotional memory. She notes that Stanislavski had almost completely discarded the use of emotional memory by the last years of his life, replacing it with the search for precise, strongly logical action as the key to the actor's emotional life (44). She would later teach in her Studio that emotional memory remains one of the actor's primary tools and that Stanislavski never abandoned it; he simply changed the way it was used. Moore repeats the argument Stanislavski made that though actions involve both physical and psychological aspects, physical actions can be controlled more easily (45).

Used in a productive manner, emotional memory, as a storehouse of moods and experiences, plays a significant role by providing the actor with a way to evoke personal feelings that should be analogous to those of the character (47). The actor's emotional memory can be fed and enriched through cultural experiences and human observation and used consciously. Moore recommends that an actor analyze a spontaneously appearing emotion, to determine what stimulus has stirred it. Returning to the same stimulus on a later occasion allows him to arouse the emotion as if for the first time (48). Sonia Moore indicates that the list of possible stimuli to evoke emotions is extensive: logical and truthful physical and psychological actions; "Magic If" and the given circumstances; imagination; concentration of attention; units and objectives; truth and belief; the subtext of the role; character relationships; and design elements such as lighting, sound effects, and scenery.

In *The Stanislavski Method*, she recounts how Stanislavski pursued the study of experimental psychology and indicates how easily the System was misinterpreted, even in Russia. Among the misguided enthusiasts who taught his System were psychologists and doctors, as well as actors. Focusing on elements such as concentration and relaxation, they imbued it with a hazy, spiritual character. Sonia Moore emphasizes that this harmful approach toward his work was not what Stanislavski intended: he wanted to help actors, not torture them (46).

In chapter 3, section 4, "Relaxation of the Muscles," Moore agrees with Stanislavski's dictum that actors must eliminate tension from muscles not directly involved in a given action or movement, providing control over them (35). (The muscles of the body occupied a place of primary importance in Sonia Moore's adaptation of the Method of Physical Actions in the 1980s and 1990s. She moved from simply relaxing the muscles to exploring them as a direct link to the actor's emotional life.) Finally, in chapter 3, section 16, "The Actor's Physical Apparatus," she notes that, in order for the actor to express the inner life of the character, the body must be trained to allow for graceful, expressive movement (72). There is no place, however, for clichéd, involuntary gestures that do not reflect thoughts and feelings (73). Here, Moore plants the seed that will blossom later in her use of the "gesture" as the actor's primary tool of communication and an essential part of an action.

In *The Stanislavski Method*, Sonia Moore makes great progress in clarifying Stanislavksi's work, reducing it to its essential elements, and reinforcing the place of psychophysical action in his System.

THE STANISLAVSKI SYSTEM (1965)

In an interview published in July 1965, Moore was asked if there had been sufficient new discoveries about Stanislavski, beyond what was currently known, that would warrant a revision and expansion of her first book. She replied that "in the past few years . . . Russian directors, actors, historians and scientists have been researching Stanislavski's writings, of which the two books known in this country are only a small part. A great deal more information is available today."[10] Though her publisher initially fought the name change from "Method" to "System" (by now Strasberg's Method was firmly fixed in the imagination and practice of American actors), Moore prevailed. The "method of physical actions is only a part of the total system of acting, which Stanislavski evolved over 40 or more years." The System "recognizes behavior as a psycho-physical process."[11] These statements set the stage for the 1965 transformation of *The Stanislavski Method* into *The Stanislavski System*. This new version was received as well as the first and praised as "the most precise and compact digest of Stanislavsky's system. . . . Very clear in its detail, and comprehensive in its summary . . . it speaks straightforwardly."[12]

Moore's research between 1960 and 1965 resulted in significant changes in three areas. First, the expanded bibliography includes books by Moscow Art Theatre actors and several Russian scientists, most notably a seminal work by P. V. Simonov. Second, the organization of the book, with significant deletions and additions, reflects her shifting emphases. She mentions, for the first time, the Method of Physical Actions and includes the term *psychophysical*. Third, the tone of *The Stanislavski System* differs from *The Stanislavski Method*, moving from a descriptive style to a more prescriptive style.

Bibliography

Though the bibliography includes many of the sources referenced in *The Stanislavski Method*, new materials indicate that she was researching works on Evgeni Vakhtangov and the Third Studio. An entire new chapter on him details his life and his experimentation with the Stanislavski System and theatrical form. Sonia Moore's focus on expressive, often theatrical, gestures, even in the most realistic of scenes, reflected Vakhtangov's influence. But perhaps the most significant additions to the bibliography are scientific in nature: *Technology of an Actor's Art* by P. Ershov (1959) and *The Method of K. S. Stanislavski and the Physiology of Emotions* by P. V. Simonov (1962). Moore used Simonov's conclusions as bases for much of her later work, and his appearance in the bibliography of *The Stanislavski System* suggests that, early on, Moore had a scientific perspective on the Method of Physical Actions.

The Stanislavski System also includes books by Russian theatre artists, some of whom, like Vasily Toporkov, worked with Stanislavski in his last years. These texts suggest that Sonia Moore was absorbing various opinions on Stanislavskian theatre practice of those closest to him at the end, as well as the opinions of contemporary Soviet artists. *Theatre*, a monthly magazine published by the Union of Writers of the USSR and the Ministry of Culture of the USSR, was also a staple of her reading diet. The expanded bibliography demonstrates her desire to stay current with Soviet research.

Organization

The contents and structure of *The Stanislavski System* reflect the complexity and depth of Moore's changing point of view. Some sections from her first book are deleted and others added. The new first chapter, "Stanislavski and His System," refers to her time at the Third Studio of the Moscow Art Theatre and provides anecdotes and a sense of the atmosphere created by Vakhtangov. She recounts memories of rehearsals beginning at eleven o'clock at night and continuing until eight in the morning. This same intense, disciplined, all-consuming approach to theatre was often in evidence in her rehearsals at the Sonia Moore Studio. In this chapter she also introduces themes that will be repeated throughout her professional life. For example, Moore reaffirms her belief that Stanislavski created a science of theatre art and that the System offers limitless opportunities for experimenting with its elements (23). She credits Stanislavski's contact with Pavlov with providing the scientific foundation for his System (27).

Moore states that P. V. Simonov's text, *The Method of K. S. Stanislavski and the Physiology of Emotions*, was the first scientific book to make an analysis of the System and to underscore the fact that physiology has proven the System's efficacy. Ignoring Stanislavski's work, says Simonov, is as perilous for actors as it is hazardous for writers to discount the rules of literary language (31). Further, Moore asserts that Russian scientists, aided by theatre experts, have discovered in the System a resource for the study of controlled and uncontrolled behavior. According to Sonia Moore, Simonov has established indisputably that the approach formulated by Stanislavski provides the blueprint for the creative process (32). This scientific viewpoint would now permeate all of her writing, research, and teaching in the decades that followed.

Also appearing for the first time is the notion that in the early stages of Stanislavski's work on his System he experimented with a variety of conscious instruments to reach the subconscious. Each of them, including emotional memory, eventually proved to be disappointing (29). Though the Method of Physical Actions was given its distinct name at the end of his life, it was not an appendage to his System. On the contrary, Stanislavski's investigation of action permeates the whole technique from its inception to its conclusion (29). Moore suggests that Stanislavski reversed the means that bring an actor into a creative state, giving the physical rather than the psychological primacy.

In the 1965 revision, Sonia Moore also introduces a theme that is repeated frequently throughout her writing and teaching: it was Stanislavski's forty-year, dogged search for the solution to spontaneity on stage that provided results. This extended period of evolution parallels her three decades in search of ways to adapt the Method of Physical Actions. Since Stanislavski did not have time to complete his work, Moore felt that she, in her way, continued his exploration.

In the chapter "The Method of Physical Actions," Sonia Moore establishes Simonov's point of view: "Paths of nerves through thousands of fibers connect physical actions with emotions and with endlessly varied nuances of human experience."[13] The notion that nerves provide the connective link in the psychophysical process would later become the basis for the most controversial and difficult aspect of her work: the movement of muscles along the spine to stimulate specific emotions. Moore also confirms that Stanislavski relegated the "elements" of his System, once its centerpiece, to a secondary role: "Magic If," given circumstances, imagination, concentration of attention, truth and belief, communion, adaptation, tempo-rhythm, and emotional memory now exist to provide support for the truthful execution of physical actions (41).

With the addition of two chapters, "Analysis through Actions" and "Work on the Role: Building a Character," Sonia Moore moves toward application of the System to the classroom and the rehearsal studio. She hints at her upcoming book, *Training an Actor*, a series of lessons culled from her classes at the Sonia Moore Studio. In "Analysis through Actions," she acknowledges

Stanislavski's change in rehearsal process from prolonged table work to selection and exploration of physical actions; in "Work on the Role," she emphasizes that the actor builds the character through specific choices of action (84).

In her discussion of the function of the inner monologue in complement-
ing the actors' dialogue, Moore makes an interesting observation that lays the
groundwork for her later technique. Before an actor can respond to another
actor, she must absorb and appraise the other's behavior, which includes the
partner's verbal and physical actions as well as unspoken thoughts. This inner reflection and evaluation results in a decision to carry out an external action (93). By the mid-1980s Sonia Moore had separated an action into a series of steps that accounted for the moment before and the moment after the
action was executed. (Her introduction of this internal evaluative process
suggests that future directions were already in her thoughts.)

The deletion of several chapters that had been in *The Stanislavski
Method*—"Motive Forces of Psychological Life," "The Actor's Inner State,"
and "The Subconscious in the Inner Creative State"—illustrates the growing
importance of physical action in her interpretation of Stanislavksi. Though
some of the content of these deleted chapters is included in other chapters
in *The Stanislavski System*, denying them separate headings seems to lessen
their significance.

Tone

There is a marked difference in tone between *The Stanislavski Method* and
The Stanislavski System. Sonia Moore jumped from a simple, descriptive version of Stanislavski's work in the former book to a more complex, detailed,
prescriptive account in the latter. This tone found its way into most of her future writing, teaching, and directing. It reflected her tireless commitment to
clarify and defend Stanislavski's System and also her distinctive personality.
For example, her choice of quotes by Stanislavski offers a rigid, often judg-
mental denunciation of actors who place personal, commercial interests
above their art. They are described as mediocre, vulgar, and superficial individuals who have succumbed to the temptations of the stage. She reminds
the reader that Stanislavski demanded a soldier's discipline in his actors without exception and without mercy (20). The image of Sonia Moore that
emerges from *The Stanislavski System* is of a disciple fiercely determined to
spread the gospel.

Two revised editions of *The Stanislavski System*, in 1974 and 1984, testify
to the book's consistent popularity over the years and to Moore's continuing
efforts to expand her knowledge of the System and to explore its many aspects.

THE STANISLAVSKI SYSTEM (1974)

In the author's note that introduces the 1974 edition, Moore indicates that the changes made from the 1965 version are the result of her research of Russian theatre experts and her experience applying this information to the training of actors. Specifically, she states that the book includes a greater focus on the actor's control of his body to enhance outer expression of inner processes; a reminder that the elements of the System should not be studied in isolation; the analysis of events on stage; the use of emotional memory as the basis for an actor's truthful experience in the theatre; and reinforcement of Moore's contention that the Method of Physical Actions is the solution to organic behavior (xix).

According to Moore, conscious control of the actor's body is crucial because many actors assume that their creativity is the manifestation of subconscious activity. On the contrary, conscious, detailed work on the Stanislavski System prepares the ground for the subconscious creative state (78). In this edition, her exercises and improvisations now urge the actor to find analogous situations from life that parallel the circumstances of the improvisation. In making thoughtful, concrete choices, the actor is able to unite simple physical actions with more intricate psychological actions (26). The notion that the actor must demonstrate management of the body anticipates Moore's eventual focus on conscious movement of muscles in the 1980s and 1990s. Of equal importance is the emphasis on the simultaneous training of both the body and the mind so that the actor can successfully personify the spiritual life of the character (63).

Once again, as in the 1965 text, Sonia Moore tackles the issue of Stanislavski's elements of his System and urges the reader of the 1974 edition to consider each element's connection to psychophysical action. For example, concentration does not need to be practiced in isolation (35, 37) and communion naturally occurs when dialogue, images, thoughts, and decisions flow between two actors who speak and listen to each other. If an actor pursues an objective strongly, attempting to obtain a physical response from a partner, the attention is concentrated and communion is achieved (41). In performing a psychophysical action, the actor automatically uses all of Stanislavski's elements.

In the chapter titled "Analysis through Events and Actions," the concept of "the event" appears alongside the "analysis of action." The relationship between the two is clear: the event is a noun and the action is a verb. In the process of exploring the play on stage, the actor experiments with choosing actions that will reveal each event, or each episode of the play. Stanislavski suggested that understanding the play was the result of determining each event, and its essence, which in turn dictated the actions (54–56).

The section titled "Emotional Memory" represents the greatest shift from 1965, providing a fuller, more scientific discussion. Her goal here is to affirm the importance of emotional memory while at the same time providing an alternative to the problem of forcing emotion. The solution resides in the physiology of emotion. After reviewing the role Ribot's research played in Stanislavski's creation of the System, Moore introduces Stanislavski's differentiation between "stage emotion" and "emotion in life." While real-life emotion is a primary experience, stage emotion is a repeated one and does not arise from an actual cause. It is stirred because the actor has felt an analogous emotion many times in her own life (49). Each occurrence places a mark on the central nervous system, sensitizing nerves associated with the particular experience (50). Not only does the actor's emotional memory leave an imprint, it also synthesizes feelings of the same nature, though arising from different circumstances. For example, Moore suggests that if the actor has undergone an emotion such as envy on many occasions, it does not matter whether the envy is triggered by a friend winning the lottery or getting a better job or being cast in a great role. The common element in these examples leaves an impression on the memory. Sonia Moore indicates that Stanislavski referred to these traces as a single, compressed, intensified memory of an emotion (50, 51), in this case, envy.

Moore embraces Pavlov's influence in suggesting that the actor is able to bring out this imprint of a past feeling in response to a conditioned stage stimulus during rehearsals (51). The stimulus is some form of physical action often shaped by one or more of Stanislavski's original elements. The recreated stage emotion differs from the primary emotion in that it does not absorb the actor completely. The actor is not lost on stage but instead is able to experience the emotion and see herself experiencing the emotion simultaneously, thus demonstrating eighteenth-century French philosopher Denis Diderot's "paradox of acting."

Carnicke notes that Stanislavski was aware of the complex nature of emotional memory. For him, "primary feelings are 'spontaneous, strong, highly coloured' and occur rarely. 'It's annoying: we do not control moments of primary experience; they control us.'" While these moments are exhilarating and illuminating for the actor, they can be dangerous because they are uncontrollable. "Thus, Stanislavski sees the avoidance of primary feelings on stage as a matter of 'mental hygiene.'" Actors must learn to "summon secondary feelings during performances . . . [which are] 'more accessible' . . . [and] 'prompt our memory of emotion.'"[14] Memory filters emotion, allowing the actor to maintain an artistic distance between himself and the event portrayed. Paradoxically, by transforming emotion into art, emotional memory "'results in the quintessence of all similar feelings. . . .' and, therefore, 'it is stronger than genuine real-life feeling.'"[15]

In the 1974 revision Sonia Moore clarifies the "gesture" previously introduced in 1965 and identifies its place in communicating and influencing the inner life of the actor. Though Moore had already claimed that a gesture must reveal an internal experience (1965), by 1974 she instructed students to express what is thought and felt by adjusting the body (36). This movement is tied both to physical and verbal actions, since words are generated by thoughts, images, and physical expressions of inner life. (68).

Finally, Moore's effort to establish the Method of Physical Actions as the key to organic stage behavior is more fully realized in the 1974 revision. At every opportunity, she infuses discussion of the "physical" and the "psychological" into her treatments of the elements, of analysis through events and actions, and of work on exercises and improvisations.

THE STANISLAVSKI SYSTEM (1984)

The 1984 revision details more completely the function of the gesture. Providing that the actor's body is trained to be responsive, through gestures he speaks in silences by communicating the inner monologue and creating a continuous current of life on stage (20). Gestures, executed before and after the actor speaks, project what words alone cannot, and they must be chosen carefully, absolutely necessary, and easily recognizable (20). In 1974 there was one gesture—before the actor speaks; by 1984 there were gestures both before and after a speech (59).

As important as verbal actions are, words cannot express everything. Human behavior is communicated through gestures, postures, looks, and silences. Sonia Moore directed actors performing improvisations to choose gestures to project beliefs, feelings, and assessments, before and after actions. This could only occur when the muscles of the actor's body were powerfully receptive to interior processes (23).

The most obvious change from 1974 to 1984 is in the chapter entitled "The Method of Physical Actions," in which she discusses her interpretation of this technique in greater detail. The emphasis on the body expressing thoughts even when an individual is not aware of them, and the impossibility of separating an experience from its physical expression are the cornerstones of the chapter (18). Sentence by sentence, she clarifies the difference between physical movement (a mechanical act) and physical action (a purposeful act). Simonov states that "the creation of the external line of the physical actions is simultaneously the creation of the logic and sequence of emotions."[16] Moore supports his contention by suggesting that every nuance of emotion is connected to a physical action.

In reminding the reader that even profound processes of inner life are communicated through the body in simple ways, such as a shoulder shrug or a movement of the torso (18), Moore alludes to her later experiments in the 1980s where she broadened the definition of physical action to include the movement of muscles around the spine. (Thus, in 1984 she is moving toward her ultimate assertion that a specific muscle must be searched for and moved in order to stir a specific emotion.) She stresses the importance of expressive form in moments of silence and stillness: the body must be almost motionless while one is speaking (59). The verbal action, or line of dialogue, is influenced by the body's gesture but does not compete with it. This idea of "dynamic stillness" became a significant aspect of Moore's adaptation of the Method of Physical Actions.

"The Subtext of Behavior," a chapter added in the 1984 edition, reminds the reader that this aspect of the System was born during the Moscow Art Theatre productions of Chekhov's plays. Subtext provided a means for expressing the characters' emotions and thoughts and helped set up dramatic confrontations with the text (69). Moore supports Stanislavski's point of view that the primary value of the text lies in the subtext (70). She makes the case that in order to create a meaningful, clear subtext, the actor needs a body trained to a state of extreme sensitivity; only then will he be capable of communicating subtle nuances of inner action with the correct gestures. When gestures do not appear spontaneously, they must be consciously chosen. Finally, in the 1984 edition, Moore defines the Method of Physical Actions as a means of analyzing a play through improvisations exploring actions. The search for a logical, consecutive line of actions *is* the analysis of a character in which the actor's mind, senses, intuition, and muscles participate (21).

From *The Stanislavski Method* in 1960 to the final revision of *The Stanislavski System* in 1984, Sonia Moore demonstrated her growing commitment to the clarification of Stanislavski's work. In doing so, she emphasized psychophysical action as the key to every exercise and improvisation as a way to stir emotional life. She introduced the gesture as a powerful tool for expressing psychological life and initiated the notion that an inner evaluative process influences the choice of gesture. Finally, with her concentration on the movement of the spine, Moore foreshadowed her eventual focus on the muscles of the body.

TRAINING AN ACTOR (1968)

Shortly after she wrote *The Stanislavski Method* in 1960, Sonia Moore opened the Sonia Moore Studio of the Theatre. She firmly believed that in order for theatre to reach the level of excellence of the other arts in the United States, the Stanislavski System must become the uniform method of training.[17] Throughout the years of the Studio's existence, she made a practice of aligning her teaching of the System with her understanding of it. In 1968 Sonia

Moore published *Training an Actor: The Stanislavski System in Class* (revised in 1979) as an attempt to demonstrate her perspective in practice. A 1969 review of her book commented that, though there had been a variety of studies of Stanislavski's System at work in America, notably Lee Strasberg's, "it remained for Sonia Moore, a native Russian . . . to give the system clarity and understandable meaning. . . . It must fascinate even those students of acting who reject the Stanislavski method."[18]

Training an Actor consists of material on the history of the System, appendixes with sample scenes and a sample character biography, and a series of twenty-four sessions based on transcripts from classes at the Studio. In this text Sonia Moore provides practical advice on solving problems that actors encounter on the creative path. Students begin with simple exercises and improvisations, move on to Chekhov's characters in *The Three Sisters*, and eventually explore their own scenes from a variety of plays, such as *A Month in the Country, Another Part of the Forest, Desire under the Elms, The Children's Hour, The Crucible,* and *Little Foxes.* Her objective is to demonstrate the Method of Physical Actions by clarifying Stanislavski's notion of reincarnation. The actor consciously transforms his psychological and physical behavior into that of the character to create the unique life of a human being on stage (xii).

The format of *Training an Actor* resembles that of Stanislavski's books: a master teacher interacts with a group of students. Like Stanislavski's students, some of the members of the Sonia Moore Studio of the Theatre appear to be talented and learn easily; others resist her attempts to push them to develop. *Training an Actor* offers an intriguing opportunity to observe actors growing in awareness of their artistic skills as they attempt to master the System while also providing insight into Sonia Moore's personality as a teacher.

Her work ethic and attitude in the classroom are amply demonstrated throughout. She espouses director Tyrone Guthrie's philosophy that great acting requires careful assimilation of technique. It implies a minimum of spontaneous creation and a maximum of thoroughly analyzed effort replicated with only minor deviations at every performance (xiii). Her indomitable will and determination that were evident when she was a girl in Russia are apparent in the book as well. In general, her point of view on all aspects of the Stanislavski System and actor training allows for very little disagreement. Though on occasion she encourages a student to present ideas on a character or scene, much of the time Sonia Moore speaks with the same voice of authority that marks most of her writing and teaching since the publication of *The Stanislavski System* in 1965.

The confidence and certainty with which she approached her classes demonstrate the single-mindedness of most great teachers. She uses an actor named "Ken" as the perpetual devil's advocate who fights all attempts to encourage him to work with the System in class. After viewing his uninspired improvisation on the single action of burning a letter, Sonia Moore, in exasperation, comments that he appears to be the type of actor who thinks that an audience should be happy to watch him sitting on the stage, apparently, for no reason at all. She informs "Ken" that Stanislavski was right and he is wrong. Theatre did not exist for the gratification of his ego (95–97).

Sonia Moore is honest, even blunt in her assessments. After another student, "Jeff," rehearses a scene from *Another Part of the Forest*, she criticizes him for mumbling, for failing to infuse his speech with vivid images, and declares that she does not believe his work (152–53). Though she could push students to the breaking point, she was not insensitive to the difficulty of using the System and to the enormous effort and focus required to master its various aspects. When "Jack" performs a scene from *The Three Sisters*, he defends his empty pauses and claims he is trying to fix an image in his mind. Sonia Moore is encouraging, admitting that she is trying to be patient and wishes to avoid rushing students through the learning process, but patient only to a point (84). Following an improvisation, "Ken" argues with her, declaring that his work was honest and that he believed what he had done. Moore explodes unsympathetically, accusing him of self-indulgence, saying that unless he can project the circumstances of the play, he does not belong on the stage (115). Moore reminded students that the problem was one of willpower and urged them to resist the inclination to become complacent and assume that they had learned all there was to know.

The structure of the individual chapters, each its own session, resembles that of her classes at the Studio. A warm-up period of exercises and improvisations to enhance the flexibility and sensitivity of the body and voice and to train actors in the psychophysical process is followed by scene work in which actors are coached by Moore. At various times, she reinforces her interpretation of the basic tenets of the System: the significance of the Method of Physical Actions; the evaluation of one's circumstances before making a decision to act; the importance of creating images and of the inner monologue (even writing down this monologue); and improvisation as the primary tool of rehearsal.

The publication of *Training an Actor* in 1968 occurred after the original publication of *The Stanislavski System* (1965) but before its first revision (1974). Consequently, the book reflects the integration of her research up to that point in time. For example, she included Stanislavski's shifting use of emotional memory from a technique that brought actors to a state of infectious frenzy to an element of the System that was linked to the actor's conscious control. When a student tells Moore that she tried to find something in her own life that would mirror the importance of a particular experience for her character, Moore clarifies how emotional memory is to be used. After seeing the parallel event from her life, the actor should remember the actions associated with the particular episode: the right actions will arouse her feelings (176). The emotional memory yields experiences that are translated into physical actions, which in turn trigger the emotional response of the character.

By 1968 Sonia Moore was exploring the play and characters' relationships via improvisations, teaching students that developing a character by experimenting with psychophysical actions is simultaneously the analysis of the play (112). Moore advises actors to test actions until they find the one that works; the analysis is a fluid activity, changing and adjusting until, gradually, the superobjective of the play is revealed. This protracted period of investigation by improvisation is actually a very efficient process for interpreting the play and creating the physical life of the character (201). Since events are the bases for the actions, it stands to reason that a good playwright begins by building important events and establishing their impact on the characters' actions (231).

In this edition of *Training an Actor*, Moore further emphasizes physical expressiveness. The life of the character includes not only the choice of actions in pursuit of an objective, but also the character's nonstop verbal and physical reaction to those around him. The actor's inner monologue is a reaction to what is heard or observed and may be embodied by a slight physical adjustment. Communicating attitudes and images to a partner on stage to create *communion* was stressed by Moore: ensemble work is produced when the expression on one person's face alters the expression on another's (107). Sonia Moore admonishes "Sally's" lack of reaction to her partner in a scene from *The Three Sisters*, saying that she appears to be waiting for a cue. "Sally" is reminded that she needs to answer her partner's question even if she has no lines (106). When Sonia Moore attempts to impress on "Ken" the necessity of communicating inner life, he is not convinced and informs her that sometimes people do not demonstrate feelings outwardly. Moore is emphatic: there is always some form of expression, even if it is only the movement of a finger, the minor adjustment of the head, or absolute immobility (95).

Even in silence and stillness, she insisted, a pose must also convey the fact that the actor is alive and expressive. After hearing traumatic news, for example, the actor should stop and decide what to do next, taking time to assess the circumstances (64). This notion of staying alive at all times on stage remained at the heart of Sonia Moore's work throughout her career, and she continually searched for the means to aid actors in this objective. She advised students to utilize the inner monologue to generate their reactions and chides "Mary," following the presentation of a scene from *Saint Joan*, for having no inner monologue as she waits while her scene partner speaks. "Mary" protests that she must let her partner have his moment. In response, Moore argues that "Mary" must not die in the scene; he can have his moment while "Mary" continues to absorb and respond to his words (169).

Throughout the book, Sonia Moore coaches actors, analyzes scenes and characters, and corrects student choices that are not sufficiently dramatic or do not appear to agree with her analyses. She reinforces the notion that improvisation is the primary tool of rehearsal whether in the classroom or on

the stage and urges students to use their own words as they explore each action (113). Away from the Studio, actors are to continue this process, finding
new ways to approach staging individual moments (155). Improvisations
end when the actor knows the character inside out, when the actor understands the character's everyday behaviors, such as eating, drinking, and
dressing. Then the character comes to life (83).

These logical, characteristic physical actions discovered during improvisations will naturally engage the emotions and images of the character
(178). For example, in reaction to "Evan's" improvisation during an assignment to force another actor to leave a room, Moore confirms that she provided him with the physical side of the action. He, in turn, must create the
psychological side, which includes the motivation for wanting the person to
leave as well as images of other people and places that impact on the event.
Once clarified in "Evan's" mind, he should be able to go on stage and make
his scene partner leave by acting truthfully and vigorously, stirring his inner
life (116).

At the conclusion of the 1968 edition of *Training an Actor*, Sonia Moore
reminds the reader that it is not enough that work be simple and organic.
The goal of the Stanislavski System is the moment of reincarnation when the
actor creates the character subconsciously and his rhythm becomes that of a
new person (234).

TRAINING AN ACTOR (1979)

Though this revision includes mostly minor changes from the 1968 edition,
there are a few notable exceptions. As Sonia Moore discusses physical expression throughout the book, some new terms and concepts appear. She
urges students to use their spine to convey thoughts and images, moving the
body before and after actions (36–38). These two additions—adjustments of
the spine and movements before and after actions—are significant changes
from 1968.

Moore also injects an interesting phrase in this edition—current of energy—in discussing the conscious connection to inner life. "Jeff" waves his
hands around and she admonishes him to stop, to remain still until he feels
the current of energy flow from his spine to his fingers. Only then can he
choose his poses and gestures, much as he would choose his thoughts and
images (95). "Jeff" pushes his body while speaking, when the opposite
should actually occur: it is during silences, before and after speaking, that the
actor needs to make the effort to move. But, once again, "Jeff" must pause
until he feels the current extend down his arms into his fingers before he
moves his hands (200). This reference to flow of energy from the spine appears for the first time in 1979. Sonia Moore increasingly believed that move-

ment of the area around the spine was critical in the psychophysical process. She presses students to adjust the torso before beginning a line of dialogue (108) and to use this part of the body to communicate mental processes after the line ends (118).

Repeatedly in this version, Sonia Moore refers to analogous emotion, encouraging students to find, in their own experience, emotional responses that mirror those of their characters. Once on stage, they think of physical behavior associated with the analogous emotion that also fits the imaginary circumstances (49). At this point the actor merges with the character, making it difficult to separate the behavior of the actor from the behavior of the character. A shift from analogous events (1968) to analogous emotions (1979) means that the actor identifies parallel emotions, not parallel events. Reflecting her growing understanding of emotional memory, this process justified her belief that a well-developed emotional memory is essential for an actor (229).

STANISLAVSKI REVEALED (1991)

In 1991 Sonia Moore published *Stanislavski Revealed*. Though in many ways it is an update of *Training an Actor* and resembles that manuscript in format, much of the text is new. Prior to 1991, she had not published a book since the 1984 edition of *The Stanislavski System*, but she had continued to read her Russian sources. The bibliography for *Stanislavski Revealed* includes only works published after 1983. This book was Sonia Moore's last attempt, late in her own life, to distill her interpretation of Stanislavski's teachings and present her final word on the System. *Stanislavski Revealed* describes her acting technique that begins with Stanislavski's System and the Method of Physical Actions and is adapted as a result of her research.

Moore enters new territory with her introduction of the explicit linking of muscles with emotions. It is here that her work becomes somewhat disputable and difficult to describe:

> My reading of Russian scientific sources confirms that every emotion—like every other mental process—is linked to specific muscles in our torso. In order to stir an emotion an actor must be capable of finding the muscle to which that emotion is connected. . . . The actor's body must be trained to achieve the highest degree of sensitivity. Once he has reached that level of psychophysical harmony, a movement of the right muscle will trigger the truthful emotion. (9)

This statement summarizes her interpretation of the Method of Physical Actions and its relationship to stage emotion. Throughout *Stanislavski Revealed*, Moore constantly urges students to move their muscles to turn on their emotions. By her admission, this is a complicated task. In this text Moore provides a detailed description of her own theories on the use of the gesture, muscles, and steps of an action.

The lessons in *Stanislavski Revealed* have been condensed and reduced to twelve, with a section entitled "Suggested Exercises" collected and included at the end. Students' names have been changed, but some familiar personalities remain; for example, "Ken" is now "Dan." There is less focus on the actors' analyses of, and work on, different scenes and exercises. Rather, the lessons provide Moore with the opportunity to demonstrate her latest discoveries.

Stanislavski Revealed describes other changes in Sonia Moore's thinking. Choosing images to create the character's world is still crucial, but now she urges the actor to stir the chosen images with the muscles and to express feelings about these interior pictures with gestures during pauses in the lines. Vivid expression of images to fellow actors will also affect the associations of the audience (34–35). The inner monologue, a key to the character's internal world, is now created by the steps of an action: wondering, evaluating, and making decisions. Moore admits that in the past she told students to write down the inner monologue. At this point in her work, however, she discontinued this practice. The inner monologue is created by moving the muscles that accompany the psychophysical steps (36). When the students seem confused, Moore clarifies: "You must not have an inner monologue while you are speaking. . . . It is in silences that you must wonder, evaluate, make decisions and gestures . . . and . . . move the muscles. . . . When you speak you must restrain your body" (86).

This process of working with the steps, muscles, and gestures is infused into every exercise and improvisation in *Stanislavski Revealed*. For example:

> Build the circumstances. Imagine the other people involved. . . . Imagine what you would do with your body—how you would hold your head, what you would do with your hands. Before each movement wonder, evaluate, come to a decision about what to do, and make a gesture expressing your state of mind. Move after the gesture, fulfill your physical action. When you finish moving make another gesture. The gesture does not have to be big, but it must have meaning. (39)

By the time Sonia Moore published *Stanislavski Revealed* in 1991, she had broadened her perspective of the System: the muscles are moved to touch the emotions, rather than the actor's feelings being the impetus for movement of the muscles (28). The *action* has been redefined to include not only the physical action, but also the work of the muscles in the search for the emotional trigger. Basing her interpretation of the Method of Physical Actions on the work of these muscles in the torso has proven to be the most complex aspect of her research, writing, and teaching.

NOTES

1. Michael Fitzsousa, "She Spreads Stanislavski's Work," *Waterbury Republican*, 1988, collection of Suzanne M. Trauth.

2. Sonia Moore, "A Reaction to T-57 Article on Stanislavsky," *TDR* 17, no. 2 (June 1973): 136.

3. Konstantin Stanislavsky, *Stanislavsky on the Art of the Stage*, introduced and trans. David Magarshack (New York: Hill and Wang, 1961), 51. Magarshack's introduction for the original publication of the book in 1950 is reprinted in the 1961 edition.

4. M. O. Knebel, "Superior Simplicity," in *Stanislavski Today*, ed. and trans. Sonia Moore, 44–47 (New York: American Center for Stanislavski Theatre Art, 1973), 44. According to Knebel, the turmoil created by disagreements among Stanislavski's disciples generated a "memorable discussion" in Moscow in 1952.

5. Sharon M. Carnicke, *Stanislavsky in Focus* (Amsterdam: Harwood Academic Publishers, 1998), 150.

6. Carnicke, *Stanislavsky in Focus*, 150.

7. P. V. Simonov, "Methods of Physical Activities," *Interscaena* 2, no. 1 (Winter/ Autumn 1971): 33.

8. Throughout this chapter, numbers in parentheses refer to specific page numbers in the book being discussed.

9. Comments on *The Stanislavski Method* are taken from *Publisher's Weekly*, June 1960; *Theatre Arts*, October 1960; *Library Journal*, September 1960; and *Socialist Leader*, February 1961. Reviews are located in Sonia Moore's papers in the New York Public Library for the Performing Arts.

10. Norman Nadel, "Exit 'Method,' Enter System," *New York World Telegram and Sun*, July 14, 1965, 18.

11. Nadel, "Exit 'Method,' Enter System," 18.

12. John Harrop, "The Stanislavsky System and the 'Method,'" review of *The Stanislavsky System* by Sonia Moore, *Theatre Quarterly* 7, no. 25 (Spring 1977). Though Harrop uses the *y* ending in Stanislavski for both the title of the book and the title of the review, Moore's text employs the *i* ending.

13. Simonov, "The Method of K. S. Stanislavski and the Physiology of Emotion," in *Stanislavski Today*, trans. and ed. Sonia Moore (New York: American Center for Stanislavski Theatre Art, 1973), 41.

14. Carnicke, *Stanislavsky in Focus*, 134.

15. Carnicke, *Stanislavsky in Focus*, 134–35.

16. Simonov, "Method of K. S. Stanislavski," 41.

17. Moore, *The Stanislavski System* (New York: Viking Press, 1984), vii.

18. Edward Southern Hipp, "More about Stanislavski and His Acting Theories," *Newark News*, sec. 6, January 12, 1969.

5

The History of the Sonia Moore Studio of the Theatre and the American Center for Stanislavski Theatre Art

If the heart of Sonia Moore's legacy is her books, the lifeblood of that legacy flowed from the Sonia Moore Studio of the Theatre and the American Center for Stanislavski Theatre Art (ACSTA). ACSTA, the umbrella organization for the Studio, was headed by Moore and overseen by a national advisory board and board of directors that at times included such luminaries as director Joshua Logan and actor Julie Harris, respectively. Under the auspices of ACSTA, a repertory company arose from members of the Studio. Moore's activities through these organizations chronicle her advocacy of the Stanislavski System in this country.

THE 1960s

After the success of her first textbook, Sonia Moore developed a cadre of students eager to study with her. This group included Moore's daughter, Irene Moore, already a professional actor. While learning Stanislavski's work, students rehearsed *The Painted Days* by John Byrne, which opened in April 1961 Off-Broadway at the Marquee Theatre on East 59th Street. According to one of the publicity notices for the production, Sonia Moore had offered a scene from *The Painted Days* at a free workshop prior to its opening.[1] Co-produced by then fledgling actor/producer Elliott Martin, the cast of *The Painted Days* included Irene Moore, Christopher Cary, Bill Fletcher, Lucille Fenton, Liam Lenihan, Barry Macollum, Barbara Lea, Alan MacAteer, and Tom Simcox. While Irene Moore, Fletcher, and Lea noted in their program biographies that they were students of Sonia Moore, the others did not. Conceivably, at this point Moore cast professional actors in addition to her new

59

students in order to be able to start directing in New York City. Reviewers acknowledged "earnest performances," although they doubted the intrinsic value of the play because of a lack of character depth or theme.[2]

In November 1961 Moore followed up the production of *The Painted Days* by directing the American premier of a play called *Sharon's Grave* by John B. Keane at the Maidman Playhouse on West 42nd Street. This production was "under the aegis of the Irish Players."[3] The cast included Helena Carroll, Dermot McNamara, and John Call, none of whom were students of Moore's. Nevertheless, this show presented another opportunity for her to get her name known in the professional theatre scene. Reports are that *Sharon's Grave* did not go smoothly, nor was it a successful show. Howard Taubman in his review commented that "the staging is as hectic as it is superficial," but he blamed the playwright for weak story and characterization rather than the director for her staging, never even mentioning Moore.[4]

A publicity notice sent to *Show Business* in October 1961 announced that Moore was to direct *Sharon's Grave*, but most of the notice was about the dramatic workshop that she planned to open in December 1961. A lengthy statement from Moore proclaimed the goals of her new workshop: to train actors in the real "Stanislavski Method, not the 'American Adaptation'" that emphasized mumbling and scratching, and to prove that it is "an indispensable acting technique for actors of *any* nationality, for *any* play, for *any* style."[5] This was the start of the Sonia Moore Studio of the Theatre.

As the Studio began to emerge, advertisements for it appeared in the *New York Times* with other acting studios of the period. Moore rented space to house the classes, first on 42nd Street and then at the Center on West 20th Street.[6] Ads for the Studio announced that Moore, a director and the author of *The Stanislavski Method*, taught "the Stanislavski Concrete Technique of an Actor's Work on a Role."[7] The use of the phrase "an Actor's Work on a Role" in this advertisement parallels the title of the Russian edition of Stanislavski's third volume on the System, *An Actor Works on the Role* (1957). The American version of this text, published in 1961, was entitled *Creating a Role*. Besides the difference in title, the Russian version was organized and edited differently from the American version and contained some different material.[8]

In March 1964 Moore received a letter from Elliott Martin confirming a prior conversation about forming her Studio class into an Off-Broadway repertory company. At the time, Martin was a coproducer with Daniel Hollywood in an organization called Never Too Late Cradle and All Company. Martin expressed the hope that "a building could be found where expenses could be kept to an absolute minimum and income to help defray the cost would be on a contribution basis."[9] He wanted to be able to work on new plays for a period "without pressures" and to develop "future playwrights and actors of stature."[10] While it is likely that Moore considered Martin's offer, this is not the direction in which she proceeded with her Studio.

Instead of collaborating with Martin, in the fall of 1964 Moore founded the American Center for Stanislavski Theatre Art (ACSTA), a nonprofit organization. A memo about ACSTA from this period began with a quote from President John F. Kennedy that urged the raising of "standards of artistic accomplishments."[11] It then explained the role of the Stanislavski System in this endeavor, setting forth the organization's purpose:

> The AMERICAN CENTER FOR STANISLAVSKI THEATRE ART will engage in translating Stanislavski's voluminous writing; continue research and study of his own works and those of theatre experts; share the acquired knowledge with American theatre people; will train young actors, directors, teachers and playwrights in the vital Stanislavski technique and other subjects which will raise their cultural level; will offer scholarships to talented young people; and, hopefully, contribute to the building of the American Theatre.[12]

In addition to receiving public recognition from her book, Moore, as president of the newly formed ACSTA, now found herself being interviewed on WOR-TV, WBFM radio, and in January 1965 on WNBC.

With the publication of *The Stanislavski System* in 1965, Moore continued to attract an ever-growing number of students to her Studio, both practicing professionals and beginning actors.[13] Moore spoke at Pace College and in other forums that year in New York and elsewhere as a result of her increasing fame. When she lectured, she often brought students from the Studio to demonstrate the technique through scenes, as she did, for example, in the fall of 1965 when she conducted a lecture/demonstration for WNYC-TV. She utilized these opportunities to further advertise her Studio.

In 1966 Moore began a partnership with the Library and Museum of Performing Arts at Lincoln Center that was to continue until the early 1990s, thereby turning the practice of free lectures/demonstrations that she had begun earlier into routine events. Although the initial number of these presentations is not known, a schedule of four times a year eventually was established. A flyer for one of the first events, on April 18, 1966, listed scenes from plays by Anton Chekhov and Eugene O'Neill, performed by students from the Studio, and advertised a similar presentation in May.[14] A 1967–1968 program advertised three of these events from October to December, and then another five, held once a month from January to May of 1968. The program also itemized the following topics that Moore covered in her lecture, topics that would become part of her signature talk about the Stanislavski System for the rest of her career:

> The situation in American theatre; why the System should be required training for an actor; the vital importance of the Stanislavski acting technique for our

theatre; the need for introducing a unified professional language and standard for evaluating theatre art; special conditions in which the creative process of an actor develops; objectives of the American Center for Stanislavski Theatre Art; Stanislavski's aesthetic and ethical principles; technique based on life's natural laws; control of the actor's apparatus for experiencing and incarnation; conscious means of reaching the subconscious; the secret of genius; Stanislavski's experimental methods; the method of physical actions as the heart of the System; building the spiritual content of a role and its embodiment through the physical and psychological training of an actor; reincarnation—the highest step in an actor's art; transforming an actor's own organic resources into the inner world of a character in a play; the Stanislavski analysis of a play; ensemble work; Stanislavski—the actor and director; exercises and improvisations; development and use of will power; and demonstration of the use of the Stanislavski technique in building a role.[15]

Through these free events, Moore reached scores of people over a twenty-five year period, many either interested in studying with her at the Studio or intrigued into reading her books if they had not already read them. Students at the Studio generally considered these presentations prestigious opportunities to demonstrate before a New York audience some of the exercises and character work that they studied with Moore. Although these free demonstrations continued to expand, Irene Moore recalls that there were no full-fledged productions during the period, nor have the authors found any evidence of productions.

In 1966 one of the students who began working with Moore was actor Jane Marla Robbins. Robbins, author of the book *Acting Techniques for Everyday Life* (2002), studied with Moore until 1970. While at the Studio, Robbins developed the successful one-woman show *Dear Nobody*, about the life of eighteenth-century novelist Fanny Burney. Robbins said of Moore that "her ability to help me develop character was amazing. . . . My fourth finger had to reflect the superobjective of the play."[16] Robbins' career has spanned Broadway, films, and television. She returned to Moore's tutelage on occasion and at one point even returned to perform with the repertory company.

From October 1967 to May 1968, the New York City Department of Recreation and Cultural Affairs sponsored a free ACSTA workshop on the Stanislavski System at the Lost Battalion Hall in Queens. This was supervised by Moore but taught by one of the teachers trained at the Studio. (Throughout the years, most of her teachers at the Studio were her American students.) Also in April 1968, "actor-members" of the Studio, as they were called at the time, participated in a Shakespeare Festival broadcast on WNYC radio. In May actor-members were interviewed and performed scenes on the show *Broadway after Dark* on WBHI-FM. A series of thirteen lectures/demonstrations taped at Lincoln Center were broadcast on WNYC-FM from November 1968 through January 1969.

As the 1960s progressed, Sonia Moore continued to attract publicity by writing a new textbook and making appearances as the head of ACSTA. Luminaries such as Joseph Chaikin and Richard Schechner created companies practicing ritualistic, nonrealistic acting techniques that mirrored the social/political unrest of the country, while Moore promoted an acting technique often deemed suited for only "realistic" acting and plays.[17] The success of the Actors Studio and the feud that still surrounded the American Method also helped to funnel students her way. Moore's appeal as a direct descendent of those who had studied at the Moscow Art Theatre continued to intrigue students who sought to study with a master. Few other acting teachers in New York at that time could make such a claim. Even more distinctively, Sonia Moore had written successful books on the System. Her texts sold well commercially and were utilized in many university drama departments, so they kept a steady stream of students knocking at her door.

On May 5, 1969, ACSTA held a successful fund-raiser for the organization entitled "An Evening with Sonia Moore" in the Studio's space on West 20th Street. As part of the program, students from the Studio presented one-acts and scenes from plays by Chekhov, Tennessee Williams, William Saroyan, and others. From a letter by Mrs. Herbert Brownell, a member of the national advisory board of ACSTA, to contributors:

> Our goal is to raise funds for the founding of the first American repertory company composed of actors trained in the up-to-date Stanislavski professional acting technique. A school which will continuously provide actors trained in the Stanislavski System and capable of ensemble work, will be attached.[18]

This was the official launching of the repertory company and, potentially, of the full-time school that Sonia Moore aimed to found in America, similar to the model provided by the Moscow Art Theatre.[19] A *Back Stage* review of the event singled out a few performers, for example, Irene Moore in her "impressive performance" of Garcia Lorca's eponymous character Yerma. It also noted that although "too many actors and pieces to mention each individually were presented . . . the quality of the performances was generally good, with occasional lapses in time and in accents."[20] Moore, of course, had directed two productions in New York City by this time and had presented numerous scenes with students throughout the metropolitan area. Her repertory company would surface for the first time in the fall of 1970, and it would eventually garner more favorable publicity for Moore's advocacy of Stanislavski's work.

THE 1970s

In February 1970 two of the actor-members of the Studio, Philip G. Bennett and Dolores Brandon Walker, spearheaded a campaign to acquire funding for the newly proposed repertory company. In a letter entitled "Proposal for Aid" and addressed to future patrons, they outlined the past accomplishments and future undertakings of ACSTA and Sonia Moore, noting that "the American Center is the only organization outside the Iron Curtain countries equipped to bring the conclusive deductions of Stanislavski to America."[21] The goals set forth in this appeal matched many of Moore's lecture topics, for example, "to reform the American theatre artistically and ethically . . . to introduce America to true ensemble theatre . . . to establish a theatre of dignity and idealism," and to make the Stanislavski System "required preparation for all actors."[22]

The words demonstrated Moore's students' dedication to achieving objectives she originated and they are written with a conviction similar to the way in which Moore often expressed herself. In the document, Moore's handwritten note even corrects an initial statement from "We are presently working on Chekhov's *The Cherry Orchard*" to "We are ready to begin our repertory and preparation of Chekhov's *The Cherry Orchard* as our first production." This suggests that Moore maintained control over what was written and was confident that she now had a company of actors, nine years after her Studio began, capable of exhibiting the Stanislavski System in full productions. Although it is not known exactly to whom this new appeal for funding was sent, Moore had previously attempted to raise funds for ACSTA, as evidenced in a January 1970 rejection letter from the Parks, Recreation and Cultural Affairs Administration for the city of New York.[23]

The recently formed repertory company found the money to perform *The Cherry Orchard* in the spring of 1970, but the production did not go as expected. According to Bennett, their initial plans to perform at the ANTA Theatre on Broadway were derailed when a company from the Midwest changed their production at the last minute from *The Three Sisters* to *The Cherry Orchard* because their sets for *The Three Sisters* never arrived.[24] The board of directors for ACSTA voted not to perform *The Cherry Orchard* at the ANTA as a result of this, so they produced the show instead in their small studio on West 20th Street. A review of the production stated that the focus was appropriately on the actors, even with hardships such as "cramped quarters, hot and stuffy; very little scenery, bare essentials; [and] simple lighting, functional at best."[25] The critic mentioned, in particular, the prepublicity that had highlighted the uniqueness of all the members of the company being trained in the Stanislavski System. He concluded, however, that Moore's intent of bringing the spirit of the studio to the stage was met "with varying degrees of success."[26]

The company followed their scaled-down-but-noteworthy first production of *The Cherry Orchard* with a radio presentation of the play on November 14, 1970.[27] They continued to perform Chekhov's masterpiece for four years as part of their repertoire, although during those years, actors came and went, theatres changed, and other plays were produced too. The focus always remained on the acting rather than on production values.

The translation of *The Cherry Orchard* used by the company was a new one done by Moore and her daughter. A program noted that Moore chose this play for the company, now formally christened ACSTA 1,[28] for two reasons. First, she saw in the play a connection between the destruction of Russian society in favor of money and security, and America's "analogous preoccupation" with capitalism.[29] Second, she believed, as did others, that Chekhov inspired the Stanislavski System and the Moscow Art Theatre because of the characters he created in his plays. His characters required actors to have "profound thought on stage" and to build what Stanislavski referred to as "the life of the human spirit" through the choice of physical actions.[30]

As with any other company of actors or organization, differences cropped up during its growing stages and at times thereafter. Bennett recalls that some of this had to do with the fact that Moore tried to model the company on her experiences as Vakhtangov's student at the Third Studio. After spending long hours rehearsing at the sometimes frigid Studio, they would then return to Moore's apartment to continue learning about Stanislavski. But some of the actors in the company, Irene Moore and Matthew Cowles, for example,[31] were already working professionals; other students needed full-time jobs to pay their rent. They could not rehearse and study all the time. Resentment grew against those just beginning their acting careers who were eager and able to spend most of their time at the Studio, and, consequently, seemed to be favored by Moore.[32]

The Studio and company had moved to All Angels Church Parish House on West 80th Street in October 1970. The company's second production, *Desire under the Elms* by Eugene O'Neill, was combined with *The Cherry Orchard* in the Spring of 1971, along with Leonard Melfi's one-act play *Birdbath*, to form the official first season of ACSTA 1. A review of *Desire under the Elms* in *Show Business* congratulated Moore for this "showcase for the work of her students."[33] The reviewer singled out performances as hypnotizing and gifted, and praised the entire cast and Moore for a production "worthy of commendation anywhere—on or off Broadway."[34] Another newspaper article combined reviews of two ACSTA 1 productions being presented in that season with a feature story on the Studio, which numbered about ninety students at the time, and on Moore's purpose in bringing the Stanislavski System to America. R. Lopat did not believe that the "psychophysical" technique worked effectively in the contemporary *Birdbath*, describing the movements of the waitress character as "excessive and disconcerting" rather than revealing, but he clearly understood how it enhanced *Desire under the Elms*. He categorized *Desire* as achieving "overtones of supreme dramatic truth."[35]

In June 1971 ACSTA 1 also performed a radio version of *Desire under the Elms* at WNYN-FM.[36] The notice about this radio drama version of the play acknowledged a future radio presentation for the company's production of *Birdbath*, and a replaying of *The Cherry Orchard*. These radio presentations were to continue throughout the early 1970s, and they surfaced again in the 1980s.

The Studio thrived because of the company's success, in addition to the sustained interest in Moore's books. Literature listed the Sonia Moore Studio of the Theatre among the other well-known acting schools in New York City as one of the top places to study acting.[37] In 1971 the company toured underprivileged areas of Manhattan, sponsored by the Mayor's Office of Neighborhood Government. ACSTA 1 incorporated fund-raisers into their activities as well. For example, in November 1971 the company sponsored a poetry reading by Russian poet Andrei Voznesensky, along with English translations read by ACSTA member Bennett.[38] Meanwhile, Moore continued to lecture at universities and for various organizations.[39]

In February 1972 a rift occurred among students. Moore's naming of Bennett as the assistant artistic director of ACSTA 1 did not resonate well with all the members. Bennett composed a letter entitled "To Unite the Group," and read it to the ensemble, urging the factions to support Moore's efforts as they went into the opening of a new season.[40] Ironically, along with the productions of *The Cherry Orchard* and *Desire under the Elms* that were firmly entrenched in their repertoire, Moore had added a series of one-act plays entitled Destruction. According to an advertisement, they were "three plays demonstrating the disintegration of an individual and/or society at different times and in different environments."[41] The plays were *The Slave* by Imamu Amiri Baraka (LeRoi Jones), *The Man with a Flower in His Mouth* by Luigi Pirandello, and *The Stronger* by August Strindberg. Reviews of the three one-acts suggested that the group remained cohesive in production, in spite of their personal disagreements and tarnished spirits.

Critics praised the performances and the program of this newest season as brilliant and provocative.[42] Ingvar Holm, a professor from the Institute for Dramatic Research in Lund, Sweden, wrote that these productions were the only true political theatre that he saw while visiting New York in 1972. He called the plays "theater about people and conflicts with uncompromising motivation. This was expressed in the casting, in the acting style and in the entire tightness and milieu of the performance."[43] Critic Michael Feingold of the *Village Voice* prefaced his remarks about the productions by stating that he was not comfortable reviewing performances at acting studios because "actors always seem to be working inward for themselves rather than for audiences."[44] Nevertheless, he suggested that it was an "interesting repertory of traditional pieces" that offered some remarkable actors, like Matthew Cowles as the listener in Pirandello's piece. He also singled out Irene Moore and Jane Marla Robbins, who played the rivals in "Strindberg's nonsense about women," which "was nearly stood on its head (as it should be) and played from a Women's Lib viewpoint."[45] As with its first productions, ACSTA 1 continued to make a name for itself.

The third season of ACSTA 1, in the spring of 1973, expanded the previous one by including another set of one-acts linked through a theme, called Values. *The Anniversary*, *The Boor*, and *The Marriage Proposal* were Chekhovian comedies, translated by Sonia Moore, about the hypocrisies that people perpetuate in society. These three plays added laughter to a mostly dramatic group of offerings, which still included *The Cherry Orchard*, *Desire under the Elms*, and Destruction. A comparison of the programs from each of the seasons reveals that actors had left roles, even though the repertoire remained the same. Some of the cast changes could be attributed to the company disagreement, as well as to normal attrition.

In "Weekend Co. Has a Big ACSTA to Grind," reviewer Michael Iachetta wrote again about the mission of the experimental repertory theatre to spread Stanislavski's Method of Physical Actions. He critiqued the work of the three Chekhovian comedies in a favorable light. Iachetta noted that the actors' technique resulted in "robust caricature, bringing together content and form" that lent credence to Moore's purpose of puncturing false values held by society.[46] Moore also kept forwarding the group's goal of community involvement; for example, by offering specially priced matinees to senior citizens through the Mayor's West Side Office of the Aging. She presented free scenes in Central Park of Arthur Miller's *The Crucible*, their newest show slated for the upcoming season.[47] In April 1973 the company performed the Values plays on WNYC-AM.[48]

A letter from Moore to Patrick McGinnis, director of operations at Philharmonic Hall at Lincoln Center, in January 1973, indicated that Lincoln Center had solicited ACSTA 1 to submit material for possible performances there the following year. The letter summarized the third season, beginning in February, as including four productions. This was an enlarged presentation apparently because of an increased grant from the New York State Council on the Arts, which had supplied them with funds in the two previous years.[49] It described the planned fourth season, as well as the purpose of the group. This collaboration did not occur, however, because as flyers displayed, the fourth season of ACSTA took place in their new home at the Greenwich Mews Theatre on West 13th Street.

This connection to Lincoln Center was the second opportunity for Moore's group to expand into something larger and more permanent, the first being the offer from Elliott Martin. Although there is no formal documentation, a third prospect also emerged. Bennett stated that around this same time, 1973–1974, the company was invited to join a new group owned by a woman from Texas called the Manhattan Theatre Club. Bennett said that when Moore asked him what he thought about the idea, he responded, "I don't know. You have to walk past a bar. Is that the kind of atmosphere we want?"[50] Moore turned down yet another offer, perhaps still not wanting to relinquish control of her Studio and company.

A perusal of the programs from the 1973 to the 1974 season shows an even larger change of actors in the plays that remained in the repertoire. Letters from Moore to Bennett, written in the summer of 1973 while she was away, indicate how greatly she relied on him to run rehearsals for the upcoming shows as well as to figure out cast changes. The 1974 season no longer included *The Cherry Orchard* but did incorporate a production of *The Crucible* and an original work by American playwright Joseph Baldwin. This play, *A Deed from the King of Spain*, was about a family in the Southwest coping with a loss of wealth and status. A letter to Moore from the author commended the cuts that she had made in his script, explained the atmosphere and sound necessary to realize the East Texas locale of his play, and theorized about the use of lighting to enhance the production.[51] In December 1973 ACSTA received a grant from the Sam S. Schubert Foundation to "assist the repertory company in its fulfillment of its many worthwhile purposes" as it was to embark on its fourth season.[52]

The 1974 spring season kept ACSTA 1 in the forefront of the Off-Off Broadway theatre scene. In *A Deed from the King of Spain*, critics praised what Moore and her students had accomplished in premiering the play.[53] Howard Thompson from the *New York Times* wrote, "A visit to the ACSTA unit . . . is a tingling refresher course in what theater is really all about."[54] He stated that Baldwin's *Deed* "simmers like a Chekhovian chamber work, then boils into a darkly sardonic symphony" under the direction of Moore and the acting of her students. Another review in *Show Business* indicted the play for reworking the Electra theme in clichés, but nevertheless admitted that "it magically works again" with flowing language, "brisk and exact staging," and riveting performances by the troupe.[55] In *The Villager*, David Sears proclaimed that ACSTA 1 was "sure to gain a reputation for being an excellent Village repertory company," as he praised how Moore subdued confrontations until "underlying passions" broke through "the action to reveal performances of depth and excitement" in *Deed*.[56]

The other new production that the company added to the 1974 season was *The Crucible*. With its "spider's web projected on the back wall," critic Emory Lewis wrote that the production was "brilliantly staged." He commented that Moore understood "the crooked line" that led "from McCarthyism to Watergate," and gave the play a "fierce urgency" through the varying acting skills of her students.[57]

While the company continued to perform, the Studio also maintained other ways of promoting itself. In addition to the continuing lecture/demonstration series at Lincoln Center, Moore also conducted an evening of Open Scenes for students who completed their second term of study. For example, on June 3, 1974, nineteen students performed scenes from plays ranging from *The Madwoman of Chaillot* to *The Zoo Story* at the Greenwich Mews Theatre. The *New York Times* reported on May 26, 1974, that the company presented scenes from O'Neill's *Desire under the Elms* in the apartment of Mrs. Herbert Brownell as part of a benefit for ACSTA.[58]

In the 1974–1975 season, ACSTA 1 began producing shows in the fall in addition to the spring of the following year. As a result of their expanded season, they increased their offerings to seven productions. Besides carrying over *The Cherry Orchard*, *The Crucible*, *A Deed from the King of Spain*, *Desire under the Elms*, and the Values and Destruction plays—each of these standards having many new cast members—they now added Harold Pinter's *The Birthday Party*. The Pinter play was a directorial project by Len Silver, a student, and it represented one of the few times that Moore did not direct the company's entire season.[59]

A review for the production of *The Cherry Orchard* praised individual performances but criticized the production overall for its "symbolic interpretation and slipshod characterization."[60] On the other hand, a review of *The Crucible*, broadcast over WHN Radio, raved about the austere production, which caused the audience to feel unprotected and vulnerable as it referenced present times.[61] Controversy about the lack of critical coverage of the group's work, in addition to certain reviews that apparently compared current productions to past ones in a less than favorable light, seemed to surface during this season. One of the students, Linda S. Chapman, wrote a letter for the *New York Times* about the critics' neglect of ACSTA 1 productions. She indicated that the company had extended performances to accommodate reviewers but to no avail, because critics wanted to see newer plays. Chapman elaborated on the group's purpose—"to show the value of the Stanislavski System in the finest plays ever written"—in order to examine and expand American culture.[62] Clearly, the company had come upon more difficult times. The letter claimed that audiences continued to attend ACSTA 1 shows but that the lack of "constructive public criticism" hindered them from assessing their effectiveness.

In November 1975 Mrs. Herbert Brownell and a committee announced that they had completed a cookbook of favorite recipes to be sold to raise money for ACSTA. The recipes and menus were from friends, celebrities, wives of past U.S. presidents, and "our present First Lady!"[63] There is no evidence of community work being done by the repertory company at this time, but Moore still lectured at universities and to professional organizations, and undertook revisions of her books. The Studio continued to attract pupils, hold classes, offer Open Scene nights, and present scenes and exercises at Lincoln Center.

For the 1975–1976 season, ACSTA 1 sought to connect to the Bicentennial celebration of the country by offering American plays only, rather than their usual mixed fare of European and American plays. The season included *A Deed from the King of Spain, Desire under the Elms, The Crucible,* and plays new to their repertoire. The additions were Tennessee Williams's classic tragedy *A Streetcar Named Desire* and "An Evening of One-Acters" that comprised *The Slave* by Imamu Amiri Baraka, *The Indian Wants the Bronx* by Israel Horovitz, and *This Property Is Condemned,* also by Williams. Controversy erupted over the direction of *The Indian Wants the Bronx,* initially intended to be directed by Len Silver, but then taken over by Moore. A letter from fellow students to Moore and the board of directors demanded that Silver be reinstated as the director or they would refuse to perform the evening of one-acts.[64] The issue of Moore's total control of the group's work surfaced again with this incident. Silver stated that there was a conflict between his approach to the play and that of Moore.[65] Ultimately, he did direct the play.

Reviews for that season seemed sparse. One in the *Village Voice* called *A Deed from the King of Spain* a "moralistic melodrama" that even the "earnestness" of the ACSTA 1 group could not save.[66] On the other hand, a review in the *Eastside Courier* claimed that their production of *A Streetcar Named Desire* made one forget the masterpiece of a movie with Marlon Brando and Vivien Leigh, for at least the night.[67] The reviewer noted that while the performances were not flawless, they, along with Moore's sense of the theatrical, matched the demands of the classic.

Meanwhile, a brochure for the Studio indicated that the faculty included four former students, plus Moore, and two teachers of speech and movement. Whatever problems ACSTA 1 had regarding the artistic aspects of productions, a lack of reviews, or internal conflicts, Studio enrollment remained steady. Evidence indicates that Moore added a series of lectures to her schedule, called "Five Talks on K. Stanislavski's Final Deductions," on Monday afternoons in the fall of 1975 with students from the repertory company demonstrating scenes. She advertised this to drama departments in universities, as well as to actors and other theatre professionals in New York City. Also, in January 1976 students from *A Streetcar Named Desire* performed scenes at the Montauk Club in Brooklyn, as part of the Montauk Club's performance series "to help talented young performers with their professional careers."[68]

A program for the 1976–1977 season shows three significant alterations. First, the company's name changed from ACSTA 1 to the American Stanislavski Theatre (AST), perhaps in an effort to give it a fresh start in critics' minds. Second, they reduced the number of productions being offered to four, possibly a reflection of the prior season's problems or a decline in the number of the student members of the company. Third, productions were, once again, scheduled only in the spring. The season's offerings were the three Chekhovian comedies, once grouped as the series called Values, along with *A Streetcar Named Desire,* introduced in the previous season.

Look Back in Anger by John Osborne and *My Poor Marat* by Aleksei Arbuzov, translated by Irene Moore, were also added.

Throughout its existence, the company had prominently displayed "ACSTA 1" along with past production photographs and/or one large profile of Stanislavski on brochures and programs. An advertisement for this season announced "The Manhattan to Moscow Theatre Trip," instead of the name of the company, and a small picture of Stanislavski imposed on prior-season production photos. This also appeared to be an attempt to remarket the group.

In spite of their change in name and advertisements, a review in *Show Business* noted that the group's first production of *Look Back in Anger* did not work because of inconsistencies in characterizations. By the end of the review, however, the critic wrote that Sonia Moore had recorded many fine successes in the past and that the rest of the season would "no doubt be up to her usual standards."[69] The effort to maintain a repertory company similarly trained in one acting technique continued to be applauded, but a lack of reviews about the season suggests that the group may not have lived up to its former successes.

For the 1977–1978 season, AST again offered productions only from January to May. They kept *My Poor Marat* and *The Boor*, along with *The Stronger* and *The Man with a Flower in His Mouth*, previously part of the Destruction collection. They also added an ambitious production of Eugene O'Neill's *Long Day's Journey into Night*. In June a professional theatre practitioner, Crandall Diehl, directed the premier of the three-act comedy *Baby Face* by rising new playwright Joseph George Caruso, based on a work by A. W. Pinero.[70] This again was one of the few times that someone other than Moore directed the company.

In the fall of the 1978–1979 season, Moore traveled to San Francisco to lecture and conduct a workshop for the Ensemble of Stanislavski Theatre Artists (ESTA). Her former student, Philip G. Bennett, had started the company, based on what he had learned from Moore. When she returned to the Studio, she directed AST members in *Long Day's Journey into Night* in November and December, and *A Streetcar Named Desire* in May and June. Moore had arranged for AST's first tour to a number of universities and colleges that season, so staging only two productions in the New York City area was probably a result of this branching out. According to flyers advertising the shows in Manhattan, the one-week residencies included a lecture by Moore on the Stanislavski System, workshops with her and the ensemble, and two public performances of *Long Day's Journey into Night*.[71]

The 1979 tours were successful endeavors. Moore and her troupe traveled to Michigan, Iowa, North Carolina, and Alberta, Canada. Literature indicates that the demand was so great that they had to turn down invitations.[72] Letters from the universities all expressed the gratitude that faculty, students, high school students, and surrounding communities felt for being able to share in Stanislavski's work through Moore and her company. One of the letters, from Dr. Michael E. Pufall at Coe College in Cedar Rapids, Iowa, stated that "we in the hinterland are indebted to your personal sacrifice, and that of your Company for making these excursions from what is considered the Mecca of Theatre . . . out of dedication to the Theatre itself. It is a case of the Mountain coming to us."[73] While none of these institutions were major universities, Moore clearly had found another avenue through which to teach about Stanislavski. As evident in the thank-you letters that Moore received, people from these institutions were fully acquainted with her texts.

The early to mid-1970s were Moore and her company's most prolific period in New York City. Possibly, Moore, seeing her recognition in the professional theatre lessen as the 1970s drew to a close, realized that she had to find another way to keep her work in the public eye. Although she seemed indefatigable in her pursuit, she herself was in her seventies at the time. Following this tour, throughout the 1980s, and into the early 1990s, her focus shifted more heavily into academia and its professional organizations and symposiums. Beginning in the mid-1980s, she also worked determinedly to acquire accreditation for her Studio by the National Association of Schools of Theatre (NAST).

THE 1980s

In the fall of 1979, the Studio relocated to the place it would call home throughout the 1980s and until its closing in 1995, Trinity Presbyterian Church on West 57th Street. The Studio rented two floors: the lower floor had a large and a small room, and the upper floor had a big, open room that could be divided. Competition for the use of the space from support groups and other occupants, and even the moderately run-down atmosphere of the new location, did not deter students from studying with Sonia Moore.

The 1980s, while not as productive as the 1970s in terms of the number of shows enacted by the repertory company, were still a vibrant time for the students enrolled at the Studio. Camaraderie began when they entered at the first level. As some students dropped out, classes merged, eventually mingling with those from more advanced levels. Moore's presence, her feet propped up on a chair and a carton of Tropicana orange juice by her side, inspired actors as she lectured about Stanislavski's "forty years" of research, and frustrated them as she shouted in her commanding Russian accent, "Move the spine!" Although she did not teach entire lessons by herself anymore, she frequently coached actors in scenes and sat in on classes.[74]

Open Scene presentations at such venues as the Nameless Theatre and SOHO Repertory, which Moore rented for those occasions, continued for pupils as they progressed in their studies. Lectures/demonstrations at Lincoln Center and in other locations throughout the city also remained as venues for performance. A 1985 newsletter distributed by ACSTA announced the link between AST and the City-as-School internship program, which gave high school students credit for assisting with the stage managing of productions or learning administrative duties in theatre. The newsletter also mentioned that Moore was interviewed on radio station WBAI, and that AST members performed the 1985 production of *The Marriage Proposal* on the station, reminiscent of the group's initial radio drama performances of the 1970s.

AST continued to present plays as it added new members from the Studio. The shows of this decade included *This Property Is Condemned* and *The Indian Wants the Bronx* (1981); *Desire under the Elms*, and *The Dumbwaiter* and *The Marriage Proposal* (1982); *The Cherry Orchard* (1983); *The Lower Depths* (1984); *The Marriage Proposal*, *The Stronger*, and *The Dumbwaiter* (1985); *Look Back in Anger* (1986); and *Anna Christie* (1989).[75] Reviews for these productions, although positive for the most part, were scarce. For example, the one-acts by Pinter and Chekhov, performed in 1982 at V.A. Smith's Chapel Theatre on West 20th Street, were reviewed in a source called *Phoenix* and in one by the name of *Seawanhaka*. In *Phoenix*, Larry Flick raved about the "startling depth and realism" of the characters in *The Dumbwaiter* but disliked the infantile fighting that formed the plot of *The Marriage Proposal*.[76] In *Seawanhaka*, Linda Gimbel commended the acting in both productions.[77] Also in that paper, Laura Barrett reported that the two main actors in the production of *Desire under the Elms*, performed a month before the one-acts, saved the show, which suffered from the "aural assault" of the New England dialect that most of the actors tried to affect.[78]

A publicity flyer for the company compiled brief excerpts of reviews from some of their shows. Included on that notice were ones from the *N.Y. Theatre Voice* and the *East Villager* for the 1984 production of *The Lower Depths* performed at the TOMI Theatre on West 83rd Street. The *N.Y. Theatre Voice* referred to Maxim Gorki's play as appropriately "bitter," and approved of the "catacomb" suggested by the basement apartment set, as well as the ways in which many of Moore's students were "shown in excellent advantage."[79] The *East Villager* called it "a wonderful fait accompli," and appreciated Moore's session after one of the shows in which she demonstrated exercises and lectured about the "Ultimate Method."[80] As in previous years, the reviews also often mentioned Moore's mission to spread Stanislavski's System and critiqued how the technique either worked or did not. These opportunities to perform Off-Off Broadway, in addition to Moore's reputation, still drew students seeking to learn acting in New York City to the Studio.

Tours by Moore with members of AST continued into the 1980s, although they were not as ambitious in their destinations as the tour in 1979. In 1980, for example, Moore took students to New England. They enacted two previously produced one-acts, *The Indian Wants the Bronx* and *This Property Is Condemned*. Also, in 1982 they traveled to Kutztown State College (now Kutztown University) in Pennsylvania, where AST members performed *The Dumbwaiter* and *The Marriage Proposal*, and Moore conducted workshops and lectures.

The 1980 tour included a sister and brother, Elizabeth and Vincent D'Onofrio. Elizabeth remembers especially Moore's dedication to the Stanislavski System and her focus on physical action. In an interview with the authors, she spoke about how her director father had arranged for Vincent and herself to study with Moore.[81] She credited Moore with being the catalyst that inspired her to read voraciously about acting and acting techniques. Elizabeth also noted that the internal work she and her brother had done with Sharon Chatton at the Actors Studio, following their time at the Sonia Moore Studio of the Theatre, enhanced the skills that they had learned initially from Moore.[82]

Vincent D'Onofrio, who plays the quirky Detective Goren on the hit NBC show *Law and Order: Criminal Intent*, is at present the most well-known actor to have emerged from the Sonia Moore Studio. He has performed on stage—for example, in 1983 on Broadway in Shirley Lauro's *Open Admissions*—and in approximately fifty-two films. Some of his most outstanding characters include the heavy private in Stanley Kubrick's *Full Metal Jacket* (1987) and the serial killer in *The Cell* (2000).[83] D'Onofrio is recognized for his development of unusual characters. He bases the execution of all his roles on the physical research that he learned at the Studio, "There is no other way to do what I do as far as I'm concerned."[84] Moore spoke of D'Onofrio's growing success with pride. It was reported, however, that when asked what stars had come out of her Studio, Moore responded, "We do not make stars, we make actors. We train actors."[85]

Sonia Moore's most significant increase of activity during the 1980s was her travel to universities, where she conducted workshops and lectures throughout North America. An article from the *Winnipeg Free Press* in March 1981 indicated that she taught at the University of Winnipeg, the Manitoba Theatre Workshop, and at a theatre company called Interact.[86] She stated that her goal was to "establish a degree-granting theatre faculty at an American university that would instruct entirely in the Stanislavski technique." This shift in objective from creating an independent conservatory to merging her Studio with a university theatre program perhaps explains her increase in efforts to teach at universities. In the fall of 1981 she spent a semester as a visiting professor at the University of Missouri, Kansas City. Moore elaborated on her desire for a university connection in an interview in 1984, prior to a visit to Franklin and Marshall College in Pennsylvania. She remarked that, instead of a relationship with one university, she now thought that "a network of schools" capable of teaching Stanislavski's "international language" was necessary.[87] Some of the other schools visited by Moore during the 1980s were Palm Beach Junior College; New York University; Trinity College in Hartford, Connecticut; and the University of North Carolina, Greensboro.[88] In addition to visits to colleges, as well as to high schools, Moore made numerous presentations at professional educational organizations, such as the Association for Theatre in Higher Education. She also spoke at the meetings of other national organizations and at international symposiums, such as "Theatre USSR: Revolution and Tradition" held at the University of South Carolina, Columbia.[89]

While Moore traveled for her cause she relied on her acting teachers to keep the Studio going. Frone Lund, another former student, instructed at the Studio from the mid-1970s until the mid-1980s. Lund urged students to pay meticulous attention to circumstances and the internal life of characters through actions. Lund has expressed gratitude for what she learned at the Studio and for the opportunities Sonia Moore gave her to perform and to teach.[90] She admired Moore for her perseverance and for what she had accomplished. However, she noted that at times it was difficult for students to grasp Moore's concepts and to put them into practice.

Lev Shekhtman also taught acting and directing at the Studio beginning in 1979. He had come from Leningrad, Russia, as a director, and provided a good contrast to the precision of Lund and to Moore's doctrinaire approach to classroom training. Shekhtman, a more flexible teacher, was also an ambitious director who felt hampered by Moore's iron-handed control over the Studio and repertory company. In 1982 Shekhtman formed his own group, Theater in Action, from some of the actors at the Studio. Not unlike the students who left Moore in the 1970s, many of them also saw no performance opportunities at the Studio beyond classes. Shekhtman, on the other hand, offered them active roles in a new company.[91] When Moore found out about this, she felt betrayed. The Studio continued to attract students through Moore's books and appearances in spite of this splinter group.

Boris Leskin, a Russian actor who taught at the Studio from the mid-1980s until the early 1990s, continued to provide a contrast to Sonia Moore's style of teaching. Leskin conducted acting training with a more lenient approach. He had an active film career before and during his time at the Studio, with roles in such films as *The Falcon and the Snowman* with Sean Penn and Timothy Hutton, and *Cadillac Man* with Robin Williams. Leskin later taught at New York University in the School of Theatre and Film.[92]

Moore reached out for funding, hiring publicity personnel and office managers throughout the years to augment her personal financial investment in ACSTA and the Studio. She made bold attempts to bring in celebrities for promotional purposes in the 1980s in particular. In 1984, for example, she awarded the First Stanislavski Excellence Award to Joshua Logan at a reception at Sardi's in New York City. In 1986 this award went to Russian dancer Natalya Makarova, also a member of the ACSTA National Advisory Board.[93] In April 1985 actor Julie Harris performed a special presentation of her Broadway hit *The Belle of Amherst* to benefit ACSTA. Harris also interviewed Moore for a video called *Stanislavski's Final Technique: Solution to Spontaneity on Stage.*[94]

In the first half of the 1980s, the number of students remained steady, with classes filled. By the last couple of years, fewer pupils from each starting class continued at the Studio. Ironically, it was in 1987 that Moore attained accreditation in the National Association of Schools of Theatre, offering a Certificate Program in Actor Training.[95] Teachers were given official attendance sheets and progress reports to fill out for each student as part of the record-keeping process. Moore believed that accreditation would help to maintain the Studio's appeal, continue to validate her work in the academic community, and perhaps, even sustain the Studio after she no longer could.

THE 1990s

The only AST production in this decade was *A View from the Bridge* by Arthur Miller in 1990. The number of students and classes offered at the Studio was minimal after this. Moore continued to offer her lectures/workshops at Lincoln Center a few more times. Clearly though, the time had arrived for her to find alternative means to ensure the perpetuity of her life's work by handing over control of the Studio. She offered Anatoly Smeliansky, head of the Moscow Art Theatre School and associate artistic director of the Moscow Art Theatre, the artistic leadership. In a letter written on July 29, 1992, he agreed to accept the position of artistic director of ACSTA.[96] Smeliansky, however, never assumed an active role in the operation. After Moore's death in May 1995 the Studio officially closed its doors at the end of the spring term in June 1995.

Ultimately, Moore's hope was to utilize the Studio and ACSTA 1/AST as a prototype for a full-time school and repertory company dedicated to training students in the Stanislavski System. Although successful in her efforts to spread Stanislavski's technique, she was not able to sustain these organizations beyond her passing. Nevertheless, their existence, and the heart that Moore infused into each of them for thirty-five years, remains an important part of her legacy.

NOTES

1. Throughout her career, Moore would continue this practice of presenting scenes rehearsed in classes as part of her free lecture series, and then turning them into full productions. Lewis Funke, "News of the Rialto Industry," *New York Times,* April 2, 1961, nytimes.com (accessed June 3, 2003).

2. Howard Taubman, review of *The Painted Days*, by John Byrne, directed by Sonia Moore, New York, *New York Times*, April 7, 1961, nytimes.com (accessed June 3, 2003).

3. Nat Dorfman to Leo Shull, October 19, 1961, Sonia Moore Papers, New York Public Library for the Performing Arts.

4. Howard Taubman, review of *Sharon's Grave*, by John B. Keane, directed by Sonia Moore, the Irish Players, New York, *New York Times*, November 9, 1961, nytimes.com (accessed Nov. 14, 2004).

5. Dorfman to Shull, October 19, 1961, Sonia Moore Papers, New York Public Library for the Performing Arts.

6. Throughout the Studio's history, Moore rented spaces all over the city.

7. *New York Times*, September 22, 1963, nytimes.com (accessed June 10, 2003).

8. Sharon M. Carnicke, *Stanislavsky in Focus* (Amsterdam: Harwood Academic Publishers, 1998), 73.

9. Elliott Martin to Sonia Moore, March 16, 1964, American Center for Stanislavski Theatre Art Papers, New York Public Library for the Performing Arts.

10. Martin to Moore.

11. Memorandum, December 15, 1964, American Center for Stanislavski Theatre Art Papers, New York Public Library for the Performing Arts.

12. Memorandum.

13. The 1965 textbook also was released in Canada, England, and Denmark by Viking Press, aiding in Moore's international appeal. In 1963 she also wrote an article to celebrate the centennial of Stanislavski's birth, for London's *The Stage and Television Today*. Sonia Moore, "Konstantin Stanislavski," *The Stage and Television Today*, January 17, 1963, 14.

14. Program, American Center for Stanislavski Theatre Art Papers, New York Public Library for the Performing Arts.

15. Program, American Center for Stanislavski Theatre Art Papers.

16. In 1995 Robbins was commissioned by the Kennedy Center to develop another one-woman show, *Reminiscences of Mozart by His Sister*. She said that she still used some of the acting techniques taught to her by Sonia Moore for that show. Jane Marla Robbins, interview by the authors, September 22, 2002.

17. The label of realistic acting plagued Stanislavski himself. By directing expressionistic plays, operas, and other styles at the MAT, he tried to prove that his technique worked for all acting styles. Moore sought to affirm the organic necessity of Stanislavski's technique also, both at her Studio and, later, in her own company's productions.

18. Mrs. Herbert Brownell, n.d., collection of Philip G. Bennett.

19. By this time, of course, the Sonia Moore Studio of the Theatre was firmly established. An advertisement for the Studio in *Back Stage* pronounced a fall term beginning October 4 and listed six teachers on staff besides Moore herself: Philip Bennett, Marcella Dodge, Zoya Leporska, Irene Moore, Bobby Troka, and Alvin Warren. It also advertised weekend teenage classes in the "up to date Stanislavski Technique." *Back Stage*, September 12, 1969, 17.

20. Tom Tolnay, review of *An Evening with Sonia Moore*, directed by Sonia Moore, the Center, New York, *Back Stage*, May 9, 1969, 19.

21. Philip G. Bennett and Dolores Brandon Walker, February 26, 1970, collection of Philip G. Bennett.

22. Bennett and Walker.

23. August Heckscher to Sonia Moore, January 1970, 14, collection of Philip G. Bennett.

24. Philip G. Bennett is the artistic director of the Bennett Theatre Lab in California and is currently writing a textbook on acting and lecturing on the System. Philip G. Bennett, interview by the authors, June 25, 2002, and July 2, 2002. The company that disrupted Moore's plans was the Meadow Brook Theater, from Oakland University in Rochester, Michigan. They performed *The Cherry Orchard* at the ANTA May 6, 1970 to May 9, 1970. www.idbd.com (accessed November 14, 2004).

25. William Brenner, review of *The Cherry Orchard*, by Anton Chekhov, directed by Sonia Moore, New York, *Show Business*, May 16, 1970, collection of Philip G. Bennett. (Issue unavailable at New York Library Public Library for the Performing Arts as of February 19, 2005.)

26. Brenner, review of *The Cherry Orchard*.

27. WNYC, "WNYC-AM to Revive Drama for Radio; *The Cherry Orchard* Slated for November 14 Broadcast," news release, November 6, 1970, collection of Philip G. Bennett.

28. Literature indicates that the company sometimes referred to itself as ACSTA I (roman numeral) and at other times as ACSTA 1.

29. *Playfare: ACSTA I*, March 1971, v. 3 (New York: Playfare), collection of Philip G. Bennett.

30. Moore's focus in her teaching had shifted to the Method of Physical Actions as the key to the Stanislavski System. This was evident in the 1965 revision of her 1960 text *The Stanislavski Method*.

31. Matthew Cowles made his Off-Broadway debut in 1968, opposite Al Pacino and John Cazale as one of the original cast members of Israel Horovitz's *The Indian Wants the Bronx*. He also appeared on Broadway. Beginning in the 1970s, he had a recurring role as Billy Clyde Tuggle on the ABC soap opera *All My Children*. Cowles has continued to act in television and films, as well as to write plays. See www.tvtome.com (accessed January 31, 2005). He is married to actor Christine Baranski. The authors were unable to contact Mr. Cowles.

32. This issue of Moore's favoritism was a problem that plagued her company throughout its existence.

33. Susan Brandner, review of *Desire under the Elms*, by Eugene O'Neill, directed by Sonia Moore, New York, *Show Business*, April 8, 1971, collection of Philip G. Bennett. (Issue unavailable at New York Public Library for the Performing Arts as of February 19, 2005.)

34. Brandner, review of *Desire under the Elms*.

35. R. Lopat, "ACSTA 1: 'Organic Theater,'" *Manhattan Park West*, May 13–26, 1971, 5.

36. WYNC, "Radio Drama Features O'Neill's *Desire under the Elms*," news release, May 19, 1971.

37. "Surveying the Top Schools: Where to Study Acting in New York," *Show Business*, March 25, 1971, 1, 4.

38. American Center for Stanislavski Theatre Art, "Soviet Poet to Benefit American Center," news release, n.d., collection of Philip G. Bennett.

39. In 1970 she began her connection to the main theatre organization in higher education, the American Theatre Association. In the 1980s this became the Association for Theatre in Higher Education.

40. "To Unite the Group," February 8, 1972, collection of Philip G. Bennett.

41. Bennett recalled that Moore always had a sense of of civic responsibility and, therefore, wanted to make a statement through her choice of plays. Bennett, interview.

42. Jennie Schulman, "Capsule Reviews: Destruction," directed by Sonia Moore, All Angels Church Parish House, New York, *Back Stage*, April 21, 1972, 16.

43. Ingvar Holm, review of *The Stronger* and *The Slave*, by August Strindberg and LeRoi Jones, respectively, directed by Sonia Moore, New York, *Dagens Nyheter* (Stockholm), July 3, 1972, flyer, American Center for Stanislavski Theatre Art Papers, New York Public Library for the Performing Arts.

44. Michael Feingold, review of Destruction, directed by Sonia Moore, All Angels Church Parish House, New York, *Village Voice*, April 20, 1972, 69.

45. Michael Feingold, *Village Voice*, 69.

46. Michael Iachetta, review of Values, directed by Sonia Moore, All Angels Church Parish House, New York, *Sunday News*, April 8, 1973, 15–16.

47. American Center for Stanislavski Theatre Art, "Senior Citizens to Attend Theater" and "Free Theater in Central Park," announcement, n.d., collection of Philip G. Bennett.

48. *New York Times*, radio, April 25, 1973, 55.

49. Sonia Moore to Patrick McGinnis, January 19, 1973, collection of Philip G. Bennett.

50. Bennett, interview.

51. Joseph Baldwin to Sonia Moore, November 22, 1973, collection of Philip G. Bennett.

52. Louis Calta, "News of the Stage," *New York Times*, December 30, 1973, 30.

53. Baldwin wrote a letter to Phyllis Gibbs, who portrayed the mother of the family, after he had seen a preview of his play, and before he returned to Nebraska. In it, he expressed his joy with the actors and elements of the production. Joseph Baldwin to Phyllis Gibbs, January 28, 1974, collection of Philip G. Bennett.

54. Howard Thompson, "The Stage," *New York Times*, February 26, 1974, 29.

55. Victor Lipton, review of *A Deed from the King of Spain*, by Joseph Baldwin, directed by Sonia Moore, Greenwich Mews Theatre, New York, *Show Business*, February 28, 1974, 12.

56. David Sears, "ACSTA I Repertory," *The Villager*, February 21, 1974, collection of Linda S. Chapman.

57. Emory Lewis, "Decades Haven't Changed Message of *The Crucible*," *Bergen Record*, May 28, 1974, collection of Linda S. Chapman.

58. Russell Edwards, "Future Social Events," "There's a Method in Their Sadness," *New York Times*, May 26, 1974, 48.

59. In the previous season, Bennett claimed that Moore had given him *The Crucible* as a directing project. He worked as the staging director, doing all the preliminary improvisations with the actors, and then Moore was supposed to come in and create the final staging. However, apparently because of a personal dispute, Moore took over the entire project. Bennett resigned as assistant artistic director of ACSTA 1 and left after that season. Bennett, interview.

60. J. P. Duffy, review of *The Cherry Orchard*, Greenwich Mews Theatre, New York, *Show Business*, March 13, 1975, 7.

61. Zipporah Mirsky and Moshe Mirsky, review of *The Crucible*, WHN Radio, May 11, 1975, written copy, collection of Linda S. Chapman.

62. Linda Susan Chapman, letter to the editor, June 13, 1975, collection of Linda S. Chapman.

63. American Center for Stanislavski Theatre Art, *Star Performances in the Kitchen*, November 1975, announcement, American Center for Stanislavski Theatre Art Papers, New York Public Library for the Performing Arts.

64. Letter to Sonia Moore and the ACSTA Board of Directors, February 19, 1976, collection of Linda S. Chapman.

65. Len Silver, interview by the authors, July 11, 2002. In 1995 Silver wrote *An Introduction to the Art of Stage Directing* (New York: Stormville Art Press).

66. David Finkle, review of *A Deed from the King of Spain*, by Joseph Baldwin, directed by Sonia Moore, Greenwich Mews Theatre, New York, *Village Voice*, December 8, 1975, 140.

67. Robert Brody, "Consummate Desires," *Eastside Courier*, May 6, 1976, collection of Linda S. Chapman.

68. Flyer, "The Montauk Club Invites You to Scenes from *A Streetcar Named Desire*," January 9, 1976, collection of Linda S. Chapman.

69. Alan L. Gansberg, review of *Look Back in Anger*, by John Osborne, directed by Sonia Moore, Greenwich Mews Theatre, New York, *Show Business*, February 1977, collection of Linda S. Chapman (gaps in issues in New York Library for the Performing Arts).

70. The program for this production listed details of Diehl's extensive career as a dancer and choreographer, noting that he turned to acting and directing later. The Internet Broadway Data Base shows Broadway credits for Diehl as the choreographer for a revival of *My Fair Lady* in 1976–1977, and as choreographer and musical stager for the 1981 revival of the same musical starring Rex Harrison. In between these Broadway productions, Diehl directed *Baby Face* for AST. Although it is not known for certain, Diehl must have studied with Moore at the Studio in order to be allowed to direct her company. Program, *Baby Face*, AST, 1978, collection of Elizabeth C. Stroppel. See also www.ibdb.com/person.asp?id=1132 (accessed November 25, 2004).

71. Flyer, n.d., American Center for Stanislavski Theatre Art, New York Public Library for the Performing Arts.

72. American Stanislavski Theatre literature, May 15, 1979, New York Public Library for the Performing Arts.

73. Dr. Michael E. Pufall to Sonia Moore, March 6, 1979, New York Public Library for the Performing Arts.

74. Among the students who studied at the Studio in the 1980s were model and actor Colette Blonigan, who played the role of Carol Heathrow opposite Mickey Rourke in *Diner* (1982); model, actor, and author Dayle Haddon, who played in *North Dallas Forty* (1979) with Nick Nolte, *Bullets Over Broadway* (1994), and in numerous other films; and actor Rick Gianasi, who starred as Matt Riker in *Mutant Hunt* (1987) and appeared in other sci-fi films and on television shows, such as *Felicity* (1998);

and Sebo Bakker, an actor from the Netherlands, who is performing and conducting workshops in the United States in the spring of 2005 with ZID Theater and is the star of the solo show *Vincent & I.*

75. The authors were unable to determine if a production occurred in 1987. There was no production in 1988. Although Moore had been rehearsing *Anna Christie* since the spring of 1987, the illness of a cast member and other cast changes because of the prolonged rehearsal period postponed the production until the following year.

76. *Phoenix* may be linked to a group of alternative newspapers listed country-wide. Larry Flick, *Phoenix*, March 1982, American Stanislavski Theatre Papers, New York Library for the Performing Arts.

77. *Seawanhaka* is the newspaper for the Brooklyn campus of Long Island University, so it is likely that this review is from that paper. Linda Gimbel, "Two Plays Baffle but Acting Is Good," *Seawanhaka*, March 18, 1982, 9, collection of Elizabeth C. Stroppel.

78. Laura Barrett, "O'Neill Play Enjoys Revival," *Seawanhaka*, March 18, 1982, 9, collection of Elizabeth C. Stroppel.

79. Publicity flyer, n.d., American Stanislavski Theatre Papers, New York Public Library for the Performing Arts.

80. Publicity flyer.

81. Elizabeth D'Onofrio, interview by the authors, August 14, 2002.

82. Based in North Carolina, Elizabeth D'Onofrio acts and teaches acting throughout the country. Her classes are called Acting as Creative Art. She is also a producer for her own company, Bella Donna Films.

83. James Brady, "In Step with Vincent D'Onofrio," *Parade*, April 11, 2004, 18. Also, www.originalvincentdonofriosite.com/biography.html (accessed November 25, 2004).

84. Brady, "In Step with Vincent D'Onofrio."

85. Francine Trevens, *Dramatics*, untitled, n.d., collection of Suzanne M. Trauth. A program from AST productions in February/March 1982 indicates that Trevens worked for Moore as her press representative at that time.

86. Ted Allan, "Soviet Drama Disciple Teaches the Method," *Winnipeg Free Press*, March 13, 1981, American Stanislavski Theatre Papers, New York Public Library for the Performing Arts.

87. Jim Ruth, "Stanislavski Disciple Bringing Method Here," *Lancaster* (PA) *Sunday News*, April 22, 1984, American Stanislavski Theatre Papers, New York Library for the Performing Arts.

88. Diane Hubbard Burns, "Sonia Moore Delivers 'The Method,'" *West Palm Beach Post*, December 1981, B1, 5. Kathy Williams, "Only One Form of Acting Suits Sonia," *Palm Beach Evening Times*, February 23, 1984, B1.

89. Moore's vita indicates that she made at least seven appearances at ATA/ATHE throughout the 1980s, and six more at other conferences.

90. Frone Lund, interview by the authors, July 25, 2002.

91. Theatre in Action traveled from one rehearsal space to another before establishing a more permanent home on West 14th Street and then eventually renovating a theatre in Soho. The group performed works by Brecht, Gogol, and Anouilh, as well as a myriad of other plays as both shows and workshops.

92. Although it is not known for certain, Shekhtman and Leskin may have been the only two acting teachers in the history of the Studio who were not former students of Moore and who were also native Russians.

93. In 1984 Makarova had won a Tony for her performance in Broadway's *On Your Toes*.

94. This video is available at the New York Public Library for the Performing Arts.

95. The National Association of Schools of Theatre is the national accreditation agency for theatre and theatre-related disciplines, setting standards for degrees from schools, conservatories, colleges, and universities. See nast.arts-accredit.org (accessed December 4, 2004).

96. Anatoly Smeliansky to Sonia Moore, collection of Suzanne M. Trauth. The authors were unsuccessful in contacting Smeliansky.

6

The Evolution of Sonia Moore's Theory at the Studio

> Your goal as an actor is to achieve the mind-body connection. . . . Then you behave as in life and imagination flows.
>
> —SM[1]

Like Stanislavski, Sonia Moore used her Studio as a laboratory. She wrote about the results of her research in her texts. During the 1960s and 1970s, Moore concentrated on some basics—defining and choosing an action; creating an inner monologue; generating images to rouse the actor's inner life; analyzing a play through improvisation; and teaching the elements of an action—that Stanislavski explored early in his career. Much of her process was similar to that described by Stanislavski in his twenty-five-point plan of rehearsal. This course of work demonstrated her efforts toward establishing the Method of Physical Actions as the primary point of departure for studying acting at the Sonia Moore Studio.

Former students and teachers recollect that as early as the mid-1970s Moore urged actors to move from the spine and to create body postures that would elicit emotional responses.[2] Philip G. Bennett recalls that in the late 1970s Sonia Moore referred to the use of the torso of the body as students attempted to connect thought and movement. She emphasized that an adjustment in thought should produce an adjustment in the actor's movement and vice versa. Feelings were to be expressed in the body.[3] By 1978 she had introduced the notion of "evaluation" and was applying it to the acting process. Members of the Studio were linking physical action with the inner monologue and were pressed to use imagery to tap into their emotional memories.[4] By the early 1980s Sonia Moore had established the use of the spine and movement of the torso, evaluation of circumstances, and the postures of the body as an outward form of the actor's inner life. As the initial pieces of her final technique were forming, Moore continued to experiment with the physical life of the actor.

She gradually developed her own process that broadened the definition of physical action and broke the action down into its smallest parts. This evolution resulted in three distinctive additions to her work that played a variation on Stanislavski's theme and culminated in her approach to teaching acting from the mid-1980s into the 1990s. First, Moore created a series of steps to execute an action; second, she suggested that the muscles of the body, particularly those in the torso around the spine, may be used directly to stimulate the emotions; third, she focused on the actor's choice of gestures to express the inner monologue and the subtext that accompany the action. In the course of analyzing her acting technique, it helps to understand the impact of Evgeni Vakhtangov and P. V. Simonov on her work.

EVGENI VAKHTANGOV

By exploring the Method of Physical Actions, Sonia Moore was following in the footsteps of her two primary sources of inspiration: Stanislavski himself and Evgeni Vakhtangov. All three spent their theatrical careers experimenting with the acting process and the challenge of creating truth on the stage. Each left a legacy. While the basis of Moore's work was the Stanislavski System, Vakhtangov's influence was, no doubt, substantial. She witnessed, firsthand, a teacher-student relationship whereby the student, Vakhtangov, adjusted his teacher's methods and material.

When the First Studio of the Moscow Art Theatre was formed, Vakhtangov, already recognized as a distinguished director, was given the responsibility for teaching Stanislavski's System to its members. But Vakhtangov questioned all aspects of his mentor's work and searched for ways of "refining and perfecting the 'system,'" particularly with regard to theatrical form.[5] He was the "rebellious son" who needed to see the psychological aspects of the System mesh with an expressive physicality. When he founded the Third Studio and directed productions there, Vakhtangov practiced his belief "that an expression of the inner life of the character must be consciously guided with precision and mastery and not allowed to simply occur spontaneously."[6] He frequently controlled actors' movements in ways that resembled choreography and referred to his art as theatrical realism.[7] His conviction that every movement and vocal inflection had to be studied meticulously was a point of view later reflected in Sonia Moore's exhaustive attention to physical expression.[8] She insisted that the actor's gestures be consciously chosen, repeatable, and expressive.

Moore describes the uncompromising discipline of the Third Studio and a severe Vakhtangov who put fear in the hearts of students. In February 1922, when he was ill with a temperature of 103 degrees, Vakhtangov called for a run-through of his final production at four o'clock in the morning, with actors completely fatigued.[9] Moore's exacting attitude toward rehearsal mirrored that of her teacher until the end. In December 1990, during one of the dress rehearsals of Arthur Miller's *A View from the Bridge*, the last play she directed, the eighty-eight-year-old Sonia Moore kept her cast into the early hours of the morning as she made adjustments in production details. Oblivious to the exhaustion of the actors, her own need for rest, and the bone-chilling cold of the performance space, Moore pushed for the creative impact she desired. The similarity in their commitment to theatrical perfection is striking.[10]

Sonia Moore's memoir indicates the strength of the impression created by the Third Studio's presentation of Vakhtangov's final production, *Princess Turandot*, which was sharply theatrical in physical form yet psychologically true. Vakhtangov adapted the the System to serve the needs of the play and its Commedia characters.[11] His implementation of the System proved its universality and aliveness, or, as Stanislavski had maintained from its inception, that it was a living, breathing entity that could benefit from refinement. Vakhtangov's legacy includes his work as a teacher, through which he shared Stanislavski's ideas, as well as his willingness to experiment with the System in spite of the resistance of Stanislavski's most devoted followers.[12]

At the Third Studio, Sonia Moore was introduced to two significant notions. First, she observed that Stanislavski's System benefited from the adaptation that it underwent in Vakhtangov's inventive hands. Second, years before Stanislavski articulated his final working method, she saw that imaginative, precise physical expression enhanced the acting process and complemented the psychological life of the character. These two lessons later helped to shape her own approach to the Method of Physical Actions.

P. V. SIMONOV

Sonia Moore's growing fascination with the research undertaken by Russian scientists to explain the Method of Physical Actions was demonstrated by her constant references to Russian neurophysiologist P. V. Simonov, particularly in the last seven or eight years of her life. Simonov suggests that his research is not intended as a "physiological substantiation" of Stanislavski's System; on the contrary, Russian scientists were preoccupied with what the System could teach them about the physiology of man's higher nervous system.[13] Simonov asserts that Stanislavski studied Pavlov's work on conditioned reflexes and that there existed a "fruitful creative communion" between the two. He further insists that Stanislavski sought a scientific analysis of creative phenomena and "a strictly objective study of the higher nervous (or psychic) activity of man."[14]

The substantial impact of Simonov's writing, and biases, are thoroughly reflected in Moore's work with the muscles of the body. Simonov states unequivocally that "Nerve paths bind physical actions with emotions. . . . Physical activities . . . revive traces of emotions lived long ago."[15] For Moore, physical action equaled the movement of the muscles. Simonov provided the scientific rationale for her investigation of the relationship between the actor's muscles and his emotional life.

SONIA MOORE'S DEVELOPMENT
OF THE METHOD OF PHYSICAL ACTIONS

> Pavlov and Stanislavski discovered together the explanation of psychophysical action. Moving muscles alone does not trigger emotions; there must be a psychological component.
>
> —SM

Moore suggested that had Stanislavski lived longer, his path of exploration might have led him to make the same discovery she had regarding the connection between specific muscles and emotional responses. While this may have been possible, her research on the mind-body relationship included more advanced information that has only come to light in recent decades. Sonia Moore's ongoing research resulted in her meeting in November 1989 with Dr. Paul Ekman, a recently retired professor of psychology who had been on the faculty in the Department of Psychiatry at the University of California, San Francisco, for thirty-two years. Dr. Ekman's primary research focused on the expression and physiology of emotion, and in July 1989 Moore wrote to Ekman explaining the Method of Physical Actions. She included references to Simonov and Russian scientific research on psychophysical involvement. Ekman's response, dated August 2, 1989, acknowledged familiarity with Stanislavski but a lack of awareness of "many of the things [Sonia Moore] mentioned." He also indicated that he had met Simonov and that their "views are quite similar." The November meeting in New York followed this correspondence.[16]

Moore was not alone in exploring the relationship between the physical and the psychological. In the 1970s and 1980s, psychologist Susana Bloch, along with colleagues, applied her research on human emotions to the acting process. Her technique, now referred to as Alba Emoting, is physiologically based and employs "effector patterns" of breathing, posture, and facial expression to create the appearance of six basic emotional states: happiness, sadness, fear, anger, eroticism, and tenderness. Although some aspects of this method of work differ from that of Sonia Moore, its psychophysical foundation is similar. Interestingly, Bloch and her colleagues suggest that in the learning phase, the effector patterns often looked like "overacting" but that, eventually, "practice with the patterns developed a kind of sensitization, so that a very slight change in the pattern was later sufficient to produce a change in the modality of the emotional output."[17] Similarly, students at the Sonia Moore Studio expressed their fear of overacting when first pursuing her work with muscles and gestures, but Moore assured them that their bodies would become sensitized to the process so that a slight adjustment of their muscles would trigger an emotional response.

MUSCLES OF THE TORSO

If your muscles don't move, it means your mind is empty. . . . The muscles must never be in repose. Make a gigantic effort to wake up the muscles. . . . Move them without interruption.

—SM

Though both Stanislavski and Sonia Moore acknowledged the importance of using the muscles to prepare the actor's body for the process of developing a character, Moore went further. She claimed that the body's muscles needed to be more than relaxed, they needed to be actively involved in triggering the emotional life of the actor. Her evolving belief in the interdependence of the actor's physical and emotional lives grew until she finally asserted that movement of the muscles in the torso influences the nerves feeding into and out of the spine that send signals to the brain. Her rationale was as follows: the muscles in the back, like all of the muscles in the body, move when ordered to by impulses originating in the brain. In turn, the moving muscles, via paths of nerves, send impulses back to the brain in a nonstop cycle of activity. These impulses, according to Moore, produce mental responses such as emotions and images. She maintained that moving the back muscles, particularly those around the spine, kept the mind and body alive.

While in principle the concept of mind-body interaction is today taken for granted, the notion that the movement of specific muscles will prompt specific emotions is less clear. When confronted with the difficulty of actually locating and moving a particular muscle, Sonia Moore frequently suggested that there was "no map" to find the correct one. A student had to experiment to locate the appropriate muscle that would turn on the desired emotion. The implication was obvious. When the correct muscle was discovered, the actor would know it. On the other hand, exactly how to achieve this muscle-emotion connection was somewhat vague.

Though Moore insisted on the subtle movement of muscles in the actor's torso, she was quick to point out that when the actor is moving or speaking, there is already physical involvement. When the actor is still or silent, waiting for a cue to speak or observing the action in a scene, this work with the muscles is of paramount importance. Nonstop movement takes great effort and demands, as she often reiterated, strong willpower on the part of the actor. Ideally, the sheer effort required to keep the body alive would prevent the actor from dropping out of the scene. Actors would sometimes complain, however, that this physical effort was equally distracting, taking them out of the circumstances of the character's life.

Sonia Moore reminded students that this work with the muscles is conscious in the beginning because it is unfamiliar to the actor. She implied that after a period of adjustment actors would be able to slip into this movement almost unconsciously as it became second nature. To help the process, Moore suggested that they visualize the spine, vertebrae, and muscles. Seeing them in the mind's eye aided actors in focusing on the torso. At times, when attempting to work on these muscles, students would shrug their shoulders wildly. Moore stopped them immediately. She pointed out that this movement was specific, small, and deep within the body and should not be visible to anyone watching the actor. Nevertheless, Sonia Moore claimed that she could see the expression of images, thoughts, and emotions reflected in the actor's face and body.

Moore included relaxation and breathing exercises in her classes. Increasing physical awareness made students more attuned to the muscles of the body. For example, the rib cage expanding and contracting during inhalation and exhalation reminded the actor that the muscles of the torso are intimately connected to the internal process of breathing.[18] The muscular movement ultimately creates a subtle vibration in the body. Though the actor appears to be still, it is a dynamic immobility accompanied by an inner vitality.[19] Sonia Moore insisted that actors begin this work in absolute stillness because the quieter the external body, the more easily an actor can focus on internal adjustments of the muscles. Moore never lost sight of the point of this work, which was to elicit the actor's emotions in the circumstances of the character's life. She frequently repeated this objective to her students.

THE STEPS OF AN ACTION

The steps create a rhythm and build. . . . Do the steps in silences. All exercises need to be connected to the steps.

—SM

While the actor moved muscles to keep the body alive, he also was working through a series of steps that precede and follow each physical action. Sonia Moore's effort to transform physical movement into physical action—that is, activity without purpose into activity with purpose—required that she break down an act of human behavior and examine its parts. She attempted to answer the question, what makes up a psychophysical action in life and how can it be duplicated on the stage? Even the simplest of actions, such as answering the phone, picking up a newspaper, or taking a bite of a sandwich, are the result of the mind and body working together. She emphasized that she turned to Aristotle for help. His writing suggested a process of human reaction that explained what occurs in life.

According to Moore's reading of Aristotle, when one experiences something—seeing, hearing, touching, tasting, or smelling—the reaction is astonishment, a receptive state. This astonishment leads to an individual philosophizing about the encounter or processing the information, which in turn results in making a decision to do something. In other words, every time a person perceives something, learns new information, or experiences an event, she reacts. This reaction is a series of behaviors that Moore identified and studied. As a result of her experimentation, she changed Aristotle's astonishment to wondering and his philosophizing to evaluating and created the first three steps of an action: wondering, evaluating, and making a decision.[20]

Moore decided, however, that these three steps alone do not describe an action completely. Once an individual makes a decision to do something, there is a gesture that manifests inner thoughts and feelings and influences the action that follows. Finally, there is the physical or verbal action followed by a concluding gesture. In identifying these six steps, Moore felt that she had defined an act of human behavior. The process that she discovered applied both to physical actions and to verbal actions: the steps were the same whether the actor was doing something or saying something. This complete act of human behavior included how the actor thought and felt about the action as well as the action itself. She realized that there are very subtle shifts in the body as the actor moves from one step to the next that make the performer noticeably more expressive. What follows is an explanation of the steps.

Wondering

As an actor approached an exercise, improvisation, or scene, the wondering phase began the process. The actor, fully aware of the character's circumstances and emotional life, was then urged to begin to move the muscles along the spine in a search for the specific connection to a specific emotion, while simultaneously wondering about the current circumstances. Moore provided an example. If you are alone at home late at night and suddenly you hear a knock on the door, you absorb the situation and questions begin to surface: What was that? Who's there? Though images and fragmented thoughts may flash through your mind, the act of wondering is physical as you move the muscles with a sense of astonishment at the turn of events. The movement of the muscles may result in a slight physical response that expresses your reaction. Startled, you might catch your breath. Wondering is a physical action that demands a reaction.

Evaluating

Taking in the circumstances in the preceding example often results in a feeling such as fear. Sonia Moore suggested that if this event were to happen in life, there might be some physiological changes, such as increased heart rate or sweaty palms. Because the circumstances of the character are fictional, and the mind knows this, you do not normally experience the same type of reaction. But as the character, you are aware of your emotional state as you evaluate the situation and weigh the options: Should I answer it? What if I do and someone threatens me? What if I don't answer it? Throughout this phase of evaluation, you continue to move muscles, keeping the body physically though subtly involved. Choices are weighed, accompanied by another small physical adjustment. If you make the circumstances vivid, knowing what feelings the character might be experiencing, and then move the muscles, Moore believed that an actor's emotions could be stirred.

Making a Decision

While the muscles continue to work, the wondering builds and gives way to an evaluation of circumstances and feelings, confronting the character with choices. Evaluation leads to a decision. You are forced to do something. At this point, the choices might include answering the door, ignoring the knocking, or staying rooted to the floor. Moore clarified that, at this moment, the character is engaged in a struggle to choose a course of action. Circumstances push the character to this crisis moment, a moment to which all previous activity has built. You make the decision to open the door.

Gesture

The steps leading up to the gesture flow, sometimes rapidly, one into the next. They culminate in a physical adjustment that seems to summarize the character's emotional state and expresses images and thoughts clearly. To Sonia Moore, the gesture was a powerful activity, since it functioned both to trigger and to project the actor's inner state. If you make the decision to open the door despite your fear, there is a physical reaction. It can be located in any part of your body and might include shifts of the torso, head, hands, or arms that project your feelings. The way the character walks to the door is affected by the gesture that precedes the action.

Physical or Verbal Action

The physical or verbal action follows the gesture. Moore reminded students that although the walk to the door is a very simple action, it should not be taken for granted. It tells a crucial part of the character's story. With this process, a simple stage movement becomes a meaningful act of behavior. The steps leading up to the walk are actually a part of the physical action. If the character chooses a verbal action, such as calling out, "Who's there?" the process is exactly the same.

The Second Gesture

In keeping with her ongoing research, Sonia Moore declared in the late 1980s that she had found another gesture. Though at the time she thought it "too complicated" to pursue, she described the second gesture and reminded actors of its existence. This "echo" of the first gesture becomes a transition into the next cycle of wondering, evaluation, and decision making and keeps the psychophysical process alive. After walking to the door, for example, the character chooses some adjustment of his body that reflects his determination to overcome his fear.

Moore was well aware of the difficulty of asking actors to break down actions into such detailed behavior and actively exercising muscles usually taken for granted. Though this work required continuous exertion, she felt that the benefits were worth the effort. Since the work is physical, the actor can control it and, according to Moore, his emotional life as well. She suggested that the body's muscles actually do the wondering, evaluating, and deciding. The steps and muscles, working together, create a psychophysical inner monologue that influences each action. Besides keeping the actor's body alive by creating subtle, physical shifts that are extraordinarily expressive, consciously choosing gestures helps the actor to eliminate random, personal habits. To Moore, crossing the arms or putting hands on hips discouraged intentional, artistic behavior.

Though Sonia Moore's expansion of the Method of Physical Actions mirrors real life, she constantly pointed out the differences. In life, actions happen quickly because the mind functions so rapidly that the steps are unconscious and not recognizable as individual activities. On the stage, as the actor integrates these steps, they should be conscious and carefully executed. Even while performing, however, circumstances may dictate an increase in the speed of the process. Moore alerted students to be aware of moments when the steps seem to collapse, one into the next, and the only visible sign of wondering, evaluating, and deciding is the gesture leading up to the action. For example, if a character hears a fire alarm go off, the inner reaction is very swift and a gesture happens quickly as the character runs to an exit.

THE GESTURE

> Every step can be seen in the eyes. . . . If emotions are stirred, gestures will come. . . .Your inner experience reaches the audience before they hear the words. Words have no meaning without gestures.
>
> —SM

The great Russian performer Fyodor Chaliapin noted that an actor's gesture is not a movement of the body but a movement of the soul. Moore often pointed out that gestures imitate human behavior. She encouraged students at the Studio to observe the world around them and to notice people conveying thoughts and feelings in a continuous stream of physical movement. Sometimes these gestures were subtle and barely detectable; at other times they were explosive and full of energy. The visible result was a mix of gestures and actions flowing together smoothly and seamlessly. Individuals talk and interact with each other, usually unaware of this movement that often reflects their personality. Though choosing the gesture is challenging for the actor, because it requires conscious performance, it also supports the actor's work in several ways. Gestures increase the physical vocabulary, communicate the subtext of the play, and are invaluable in expressing details of character.

Sonia Moore's gesture should not be confused with Michael Chekhov's Psychological Gesture. Whenever Chekhov's name was introduced in the Studio, she responded adamantly regarding the differences in their ways of defining and using the body's movement. Moore's gesture is a precise adjustment of the body that is a part of a specific action. Chekhov's Psychological Gesture is primarily a tool for freeing the body and mind (he used the term *psychophysical*) and is utilized as a preliminary exercise as an actor creates a character. Sketches of various Psychological Gestures in Michael Chekhov's *To the Actor* suggest that they are full-body, abstract, broadly expressive sculptures that are "archetypal, strong, simple and well-formed."[21] According to scholar Charles Marowitz, in an excerpt from his recent biography of Chekhov, the Psychological Gesture was Chekhov's most noteworthy achievement and is "like a seedbed from which all physical characterization stems."[22] In describing what Chekhov's Psychological Gesture is not,

Marowitz defines what Sonia Moore's is: "a psychologically crafted physical gesture." He unintentionally underscores the difference between the Chekhov and Moore.

Physical Vocabulary

> Even a yawn is a gesture.
>
> —SM

Actors need to develop a physical vocabulary much as one develops a verbal vocabulary. The search for vivid gestures forces the student to explore physical adjustments of the body that are interesting, unfamiliar, and not necessarily a part of everyday life. Though they could at first seem theatrical and not "natural," Moore's gestures eventually assist the actor in eliminating repetitious movement that is meaningless. At the Sonia Moore Studio actors were urged to cut any extraneous activity that did not project either a character's life or the story of the play and to reach beyond their daily physical behavior. For example, she frequently corrected students for leaning on "every piece of furniture that they see on stage," an activity that she associated with actors' attempts to hide their discomfort and uncertainty while on stage.[23]

Subtext

> What you feel has to reach the audience before the line or action. . . . The line may or may not contradict it. Find a subtext that conflicts with the text. The body has to continuously project subtext.
>
> —SM

In *Stanislavski Revealed,* Sonia Moore writes at length about the Stanislavski System and the projection of the subtext of the play. It was her belief that the gesture was the most powerful instrument in the actor's arsenal to project what happens beneath and around the actions and lines left unwritten by the playwright. The gesture releases the different levels of meanings of the play and becomes a significant tool of communication when the subtext contradicts the text. Moore impressed upon her students the power of stage confrontations between text and subtext, between what a character says and what a character actually feels and thinks and means by his behavior. When such a confrontation occurs, subtle gestures of the body can provide the means whereby the actor expresses these character conflicts. By clarifying the subtext, the gestures illuminate the play's meaning and the fullness of the playwright's intent.

Character Information

> The more unexpected and meaningful the gesture, the more interesting.
>
> —SM

If characters are the sum of their actions—that is, they are what they do—the gestures that accompany these actions make them unique and provide a way for the actor to project details and visual, unspoken information about the character's personality. Stage and film histories are filled with numerous, unforgettable characters whose gestures were so specific and distinctive that they etched indelible memories on the minds of the audience. Sonia Moore regularly referred to Marlon Brando and Maggie Smith as examples of actors who had a broad, often subtle, command of a wide physical vocabulary. (Though Brando was a member of the Actor's Studio and perhaps the most easily identifiable "Method actor," Moore suggested that he was an extraordinarily gifted performer who used the Method of Physical Actions unconsciously.)

WHAT DO GESTURES LOOK LIKE?

> The problem with finding gestures is that the actor needs to know what to project.
>
> —SM

"Gestures don't need to be big," Moore reminded students. Since a gesture is any movement of the body that expresses thoughts and feelings, Sonia Moore encouraged actors to work with all parts of the body, especially the neglected areas, such as the torso. She felt that slight adjustments of the upper body and shoulders could convey interior life and clarify feelings much more easily than a quantity of random movement. An actor's hand gestures, which are habitual physical activity without purpose or meaning, take less effort than conscious work with the torso. Such activity garnered a typical response from Moore: "Don't gesticulate when you talk!"

Sonia Moore fought the mistaken notion that what is believable and real must look and feel natural. On the contrary, she insisted that theatre demanded a more expansive and deliberate form of behavior and that the stage required actors to transform life into art. Once the actor is sensitized to the notion of the gesture and begins to broaden his physical vocabulary, he will find that he can use all parts of the body–head, shoulders, torso, arms, hands, fingers, legs, and even feet—to express inner life. Since there is no dictionary for this type of vocabulary, the actors at the Studio were urged to experiment and to make unusual, unfamiliar choices. For example, if a character is angry, typically she might slam her hand on the table. A more expressive choice, however, might be the decision to stiffen the torso and pound her fist into her thigh.

The gesture *influences* the line and the action that follows it. It does not *emphasize* the line. In the theatre, the use of the word *gesture* tends to have a somewhat narrow meaning and often implies hand movement. Moore's gesture could more accurately be referred to as a "physical adjustment"; however, she felt that the word *gesture* was simpler and easier to comprehend. Sometimes students in the Studio confused the gesture with the action. Both may be physical, but they serve different purposes. A physical action is chosen to achieve an objective, to move toward a goal. On the other hand, the gesture serves to color the action and to express the subtext of the character's life. Though they function differently, the gesture and the action are completely interdependent.

FINAL WORDS

> Don't push. . . . Give the technique a chance to work.
>
> —SM

Student resistance to her technique was often due to the difficulty of achieving psychophysical involvement via muscles and gestures. It was, simply, very hard to execute. Nevertheless, there were occasions at the Studio when Moore's technique worked, creating strong emotional responses and beautifully expressive characters. Undaunted by critics, Sonia Moore continued to explore her unique version of the Method of Physical Actions until the end of her life. Her preoccupation with the psychophysical life of the actor mirrored Stanislavski's own. In 1935, three years before his death, he instructed his students:

> You have an instrument of expression. You must perfect it and care for it. One cannot play Beethoven off key, or on an instrument which is out of tune. . . . If your body does not correspond to your emotions, if your voice does not carry or your hands are cramped, people will only laugh at your feelings. . . . The deeper your feelings, the more complicated the pattern of your emotions, the greater should be the expressive capacity of your body.[24]

Decades later, Sonia Moore echoed the same advice to students in her own way.

NOTES

1. Throughout this chapter, epigraphs are Sonia Moore's, as recorded in class notes compiled at the Studio from 1987 through 1995.

2. Philip G. Bennett, interview by the authors, June 25, 2002, and July 2, 2002; Elizabeth D'Onofrio, interview by the authors, August 14, 2002.

3. In his introduction to *Acting (Re)Considered*, scholar Phillip B. Zarrilli faults Sonia Moore for teaching that, in the acting process, the mind controls the body and for neglecting to explain how to embody the mental images created for the character. He quotes from Moore's *Training an Actor* (1979) to support his argument and overlooks her book *Stanislavski Revealed: The Actor's Guide to Spontaneity on Stage* (New York: Applause Theatre Books, 1991), in which, to the contrary, she promotes the actor's use of the muscles of the body as a direct path to the stimulation of the psychological life of the character. Phillip B. Zarrilli, ed., *Acting (Re)Considered*, 2nd ed. (New York: Routledge, 2002), 10–11.

4. Bennett, interview.

5. Rebecca B. Gauss, *Lear's Daughters* (New York: Peter Lang, 1999), 92.

6. Gauss, *Lear's Daughters*, 96.

7. Gauss, *Lear's Daughters*, 99.

8. Moore, *The Stanislavski System* (New York: Viking Press, 1984), 82.

9. Moore, *Stanislavski System*, 86.

10. Personal observation by Suzanne M. Trauth, who played the role of Beatrice in *A View from the Bridge*.

11. Gauss, *Lear's Daughters*, 101.

12. Mel Gordon, *The Stanislavsky Technique* (New York: Applause Theatre Book Publishers, 1987), 101.

13. P. V. Simonov, "The Method of K. S. Stanislavski and the Physiology of Emotion," in *Stanislavski Today*, trans. and ed. Sonia Moore (New York: American Center for Stanislavski Theatre Art, 1973), 34.

14. Simonov, "Method of K. S. Stanislavski," 37.

15. P. V. Simonov, "Methods of Physical Activities," *Interscaena* 2, no. 1 (1971): 23.

16. Dr. Paul Ekman to Sonia Moore, August 2, 1989, collection of Suzanne M. Trauth.

17. Susana Bloch, Pedro Orthous, and Guy Santibañez-H, "Effector Patterns of Basic Emotions: A Psychophysiological Method for Training Actors," in Zarrilli, *Acting (Re)Considered*, 223–24.

18. Bennett reported that when implementing Sonia Moore's work at his own studio he focused on the flow of muscular energy and taught that the muscles are connected to the breath. He indicated that he was aware of the evolution of her work, long after he left the Studio, and that he attempted to integrate her discoveries into his teaching. Bennett, interview.

19. Vakhtangov refers to "an inner dynamic in the externally static" when he discusses the justification of the actor's immobility, or stillness, on the stage. E. Vakhtangov, "Preparing for the Role: From the Diary of E. Vakhtangov," in *Acting: A Handbook of the Stanislavski Method*, comp. Toby Cole (New York: Crown, 1947), 122–23.

20. Felicia Hardison Londré, "Stanislavski's Champion: Sonia Moore and Her Crusade to Save the American Theatre," *Theatre History Studies* 24 (June 2004): 15. The author recalls that Sonia Moore discussed the steps that connect thought and action during her visits to New York. Londré refers to wondering as a "receptive state" and evaluation as "processing."

21. Michael Chekhov, *To the Actor: On the Technique of Acting* (New York: Harper & Row, 1953), 84. In Sonia Moore's opinion Michael Chekhov was a more accomplished actor than teacher.

22. Charles Marowitz, "The Michael Chekhov Twist," *American Theatre* (January 2005): 44. Chekhov capitalizes the term *Psychological Gesture* in his writing, while Marowitz does not.

23. Amy Hersh, "Sonia Moore Studio of the Theatre," *Back Stage*, October 16, 1992, 26, 41. In this interview Sonia Moore discusses the lack of stage concentration and the meaningless movement sometimes exhibited by actors.

24. Constantin Stanislavski, *Stanislavski's Legacy*, ed. and trans. Elizabeth Reynolds Hapgood (New York: Theatre Arts Books, 1958), 35–36.

7

Sonia Moore's Practice at the Studio

The primary goal that Sonia Moore established for actors studying at her Studio remained consistent throughout her professional career: to teach them how to reveal the life of a play and to communicate important content to an audience. Her objectives were published in her Student Handbook, as well as in her texts. In order to receive Moore's Acting Certificate, a student had to complete two years of study or four terms. Outcomes grew progressively more challenging and demanded greater psychophysical involvement as students moved from term to term.[1] The acting curriculum was structured as follows.[2]

FIRST TERM

Activity:

- Exercises and silent improvisations on purposeful logical actions that include all elements of human behavior in life, such as concentration, relaxation, tempo-rhythm, and so on (Work on all of Stanislavski's elements of an action was included in exercises.)
- Development of sensitivity of the body in order to express internal processes
- Verbal improvisations and psychophysical communication on stage
- Approaching work on a scene from a suggested play

The student should then be able to demonstrate:

- The ability to choose an important objective
- The ability to select logical actions for achieving the objective

- Awareness of the importance of the body's muscles in stirring and pro-jecting mental processes during silences on stage
- The ability to communicate with a partner in a purposeful way whether silent or speaking
- Satisfactory work on a dramatic text

Once the basic work was established, students continued to refine their abil-ities to make choices and to explore the body's muscles.

SECOND TERM

Activity:

- Exercises and silent and verbal improvisations
- Ensemble work
- Scene work: analysis of the play and the scene through events and ac-tions
- Improvisations on the character's life

This work would result in a demonstrated ability to:

- Perform an improvisation that has a beginning, middle, and end
- Reveal a clear event and superobjective in an improvisation
- Project a relationship with a partner without speaking of the relation-ship
- Create a sharp conflict
- Project the objective through the choice of actions
- Prepare a scene at a level that could be considered for performance at an Open Class
- Behave ethically, contributing to the positive atmosphere of the class[3]

In the second year, the basic activity was repeated but with higher expecta-tions for student achievement.

THIRD TERM

Activity:

- More complex exercises and improvisations
- Scene work emphasizing the building of the character's inner world and revealing it in artistic form
- Performance of scenes in class for students and for Open Classes

By this point, students were expected to demonstrate:

* Command of the body in expressing mental processes
* The projection of the subtext of behavior with means other than words
* Good control of psychophysical involvement, including the incorporation of given circumstances, concentration of attention, imagination, relaxation, correct tempo-rhythm, the "Magic If," truth and belief, communion, adaptation, and emotional memory into the actor's work (Once again, Moore stressed the inclusion of the elements of Stanislavski's System.)

Finally, by the last term, students were gaining a greater degree of independence in their work and fine-tuning their abilities to make choices and sustain their emotional, psychophysical lives.

FOURTH TERM

Activity:

* Exercises and improvisations to develop sensitivity of the body in projecting internal processes
* Work on scenes and/or one-act plays with an emphasis on choice of psychophysical actions
* Open Class performances
* Eligibility to be cast in American Stanislavski Theatre productions[4]

Final achievements included:

* The ability to behave on stage in an uninterrupted, intentional, psychophysical way
* The ability to choose purposeful actions
* The ability to analyze a play through improvisations on actions (the Method of Physical Actions)
* The capacity for significant gestures contributing to the revelation of the play's content
* The achievement of an experience of an emotion

Theoretically, the program was laid out to generate and manage the actor's emerging skill; however, like any curriculum, class content overlapped from term to term, making the cycle somewhat fluid with regard to overall goals. While it was generally true that first-term students were not working on one-act plays or performing in Open Classes, fourth-term students were still gaining awareness of the body's muscles, exploring silent improvisations, and mastering the choice of logical actions. The assumption was that all of the previous terms' material was still being mastered while new goals were established. Although the objectives did not vary significantly over the life of the Studio, emphases shifted somewhat as Sonia Moore developed her technique.

In addition to acting classes, the Sonia Moore Studio offered specialized instruction in other areas of acting training. Classes in speech and Alexander Technique were continuously available. Classes such as Directing and Shakespeare, although detailed in the Student Handbook, were not taught every term as indicated by yearly brochures. The Handbook describes the Alexander Technique as a way "to eliminate psychophysical interferences" and to reestablish "tone in the musculature that will allow the body's coordination to operate."[5] The fact that Moore chose this type of movement instruction for her Studio reflects her preoccupation with sensitizing the body's responsiveness in a very deep-rooted way. The lengthy, detailed description of the speech class in the Handbook begins by stating that it was "designed to free, develop and strengthen the voice and articulating musculature." Both classes, while focusing on the body and voice as separate entities, aided the student in achieving the psychophysical unity that Moore urged in her acting classes. Both descriptions acknowledged the significance of training the muscles in preparation for the Method of Physical Actions.

I. STUDIO EXERCISES AND IMPROVISATIONS

Before describing the precise exercises and improvisations practiced at the Studio, two particular observations are warranted. First, Sonia Moore incorporated acting exercises into all of her books. From the initial printing of *The Stanislavski System* to the last edition, activities were listed following a discussion of each of Stanislavski's elements of an action. Moore structured Studio classes around these elements in earlier years. In *Stanislavski Revealed* (1991), she organized the "Suggested Exercises" section differently and in a manner that reflected her expanded development of the integration of action as mind-body activity. This latter series of categories more closely reflected the work of the Studio in the mid-1980s and early 1990s. In reality, both approaches guided Studio practice.

The second observation is that some exercises at the Studio can be linked directly to the influence of Vakhtangov on Moore's teaching. In *The Stanislavsky Technique*, Mel Gordon includes a list of exercises used at the Third Studio. A number of them resemble those employed at the Sonia Moore Studio. In particular, there is a similarity between Vakhtangov's exercises in Concentration, Justification, and Fantasy and in Sonia Moore's class activities. Justifying three unrelated movements ("raise the right arm, put it to the forehead, put it in the pocket") and dealing with a piece of furniture as if it were a variety of objects ("kennel housing a vicious dog") are examples of exercises included in each studio's curriculum.[6]

The following list illustrates the practice at the Studio. Many of these exercises were used throughout the school's thirty-five-year existence. The authors can personally verify the utilization of each exercise at the Studio from the end of the 1970s until its closing, as well as the value of each from the perspective of students who engaged in them and teachers who critiqued them.

a. Physical Training

All Studio sessions began with activities designed to relax the muscles and release tension in the body.

1. Relaxation

- Lie on the floor and relax, raising one leg and hugging it to the chest. Release the leg, sliding it along the ground. Repeat with the other leg.
- Tense the right arm and left leg and then relax them. Tense the left arm and right leg and then relax.
- While lying on the floor, progressively tense and relax all muscle groups from the feet to the top of the head, taking an inventory of places where you hold tension.
- Imagine yourself to be a marionette with strings attached at the back of your head, shoulders, hips, and knees. Cut the strings one by one, releasing the body until you gradually collapse, like a puppet, to the floor.
- While lying on the floor, imagine your body is a balloon filled with sand. A series of zippers throughout the body (for example, from fingertips to shoulder) keep the sand inside. Release each zipper and feel body tension flow out with the sand.
- An alternate method of relaxation is to focus attention on an object, remaining in the here and now. Lie on the floor, eyes open. Focus overhead on the ceiling and describe aloud whatever is seen, continuously, for five minutes.

Once students were sufficiently relaxed, they were ready to proceed to expanding the flexibility of the body.

2. Training the Body

Although the particular training exercises that Moore focused on shifted over the years, there was always an emphasis on physical plasticity and the ability to demonstrate internal reactions. Detailed categories of activities included correct standing posture, correct sitting posture, walking naturally, walking up and down stairs, jumping, combinations of walking and jumping, sitting on the floor, speech and movement coordination, walking on a bench, standing on a bench, combinations of standing, kneeling, sitting, lying down, and falling on the stage.[7] Most activities were performed in a variety of tempo-rhythms.

Early on, pupils worked to perfect the activities simply to prepare the body for improvisations and scene work. Later, the exercises became ends in themselves when couched in circumstances and given psychological justification via the steps of an action. Directions for performing these drills follow, and they indicate Moore's degree of attention to various features of each activity and the sort of precision with which Sonia Moore approached training the actor's body. These exercises also anticipated her later preoccupation with the body's gestures and the actor's efforts to create a physical vocabulary.

Correct posture to begin work   The neck is straight and relaxed. The shoulders are down and back. When the shoulders are open, the chest is out. The spine is strong and relaxed. There must be a feeling of uplift. Stomach and diaphragm pulled in. Buttocks pulled in. Knees strongly stretched. When one leg is in front and the knee is bent, the whole weight of the body must be on the leg behind, which must have a stretched knee. Toes are twenty to thirty degrees pointed to the sides. Check the tension in your fingers and relax them.

Natural walk   Heels are on the same line. Toes slightly separated. Muscles must support the spine. Shoulders, chest, neck, and head are still and relaxed. When walking, the heel moves first, then the movement goes through the whole foot and toes until it reaches the big toe. When the step is made, the knee of the leg behind must not be relaxed.

Walking up stairs   Take a step up with the toes and the ball of one foot (front of the sole). The whole weight of the body must be on the leg that is on the higher step. Then the knee is straightened, smoothly lifting the body. While the knee is straightened, the other leg moves to the next step. Movement must be soft and plastic.

Expressive hands   Emphasis is on the left hand. Stand in a group. Slowly raise the arms to the sides, elbows slightly relaxed. Hands are hanging freely pointed down. When arms are horizontal, the hands must be at a level slightly below the shoulders. Then arms slowly go down. When assimilated, do it with arms front, then to the sides and then combine the movements. (The assumption is that the hands will follow the action of the arms in a graceful, flowing manner.)

Arms and hands   Stand in the preparatory position. Raise the arms out to the sides with great tension, stopping just below shoulder level. Release the tension and let the arms fall where they will. Experiment with first letting the palms lead, then the fingers, then hands. If the arms are relaxed they will slap the thighs, which should happen. Keep the lift of the torso, but do not tense it. Stand again in preparatory position. Bring the hands to the front of the body at waist level and circle wrists one way, then the other. Then shake out the wrists. The shaking motion must be small and as fast as possible.

b. Simple Actions: Solo and Nonverbal

Following a sometimes strenuous physical warm-up, Moore and her teachers proceeded to guide students through a series of exercises and improvisations, performed alone and in silence. They focused attention on the use of the body and, later, specifically on the use of the muscles, as they pursued simple objectives in given circumstances. Moore side coached, taking students through the steps of an action. Exercises continued to stress the elements of an action and always involved the search for an analogous emotion.

Moore started with simple physical actions that gained more complexity as both the individual session and the term progressed. At all times, actors were urged to fashion the details of their circumstances as vividly as possible. Sonia Moore's advice to actors as they began to work consisted of the following:

> Know your objective, build the circumstances, and make sure that both are clear to the audience. [When] . . . exercises are silent, the actor must have a continuous inner monologue that consists of wondering, evaluating, and making decisions. Use the muscles in your torso to stir an inner monologue. Make a gesture expressing your state of mind before and after each physical action. Never stop striving for psychophysical unity.[8]

1. Performing Simple Actions

- Pour a glass of water and give it to someone.
- Say good-bye to a place.
- Open or close a window or door.
- Pack a suitcase.
- Bury an object.
- Mop a floor.
- Read or write a letter.
- Burn a letter.
- Look through a pair of binoculars.
- Perform sports activities: pitch a baseball, swing a golf club, or shoot a basketball.

Simple actions could be adjusted to match a change in circumstances.

- Walk across the room to meet a long-lost friend. Walk across the room to answer a knock at the door, which interrupts important work.
- Stand up to recite poetry you should have memorized but did not. Stand up to cheer your winning team to victory.

- Take four steps forward on treacherous ground to rescue a child. Take four steps backward to avoid a threatening figure.
- Open a window to wave to a friend. Open a window to let smoke out of a room.
- Close a window because a tornado is blowing. Close a window to hide the fact that you are home.
- Walk the floor to quiet the noisy neighbors downstairs. Walk the floor to kill a bug.
- Hang a picture on a wall that was a gift from a friend. Hang a picture on a wall that you are obligated to keep.

Variations on these exercises required the actor to create body sculptures and stretch the imagination. Teachers reminded students to keep the inner monologue active by working through the steps and choosing expressive gestures.

- Run and freeze: jog around the space, stopping in a full-body sculpture at the word "freeze." Justify the pose by creating circumstances and actively pursue a simple physical objective.
- Create a body sculpture and apply circumstances to justify it. Pursue an objective.
- With a partner, create inanimate objects in conflict.
- Connect any three physical actions—for example, standing on a chair, kneeling on the floor, and running out of a room—and justify them; for example, stand on the chair to change a light bulb, go down on your knees to clean up the bulb after it drops, and run out of the room for a bandage because you cut your finger.

2. Using Sense Memory

Actors at the Studio practiced the recreation of preserved memories and sensations from real life. Sonia Moore frequently asserted that sense memory was a significant tool of the imagination and influenced the emotional memory. With precision, actors were asked to do the following:

- Remember a pounding headache, a freezing-cold morning, a steamy evening after a rain shower.
- Imagine the smell and feel of wet wool.
- Examine an imaginary object, such as an antique crystal bowl, feeling its weight, size, texture, and shape.
- Imagine being on a beach, feeling hot sand, and exploring sounds, sights, smells, and tastes.

- Imagine lifting and moving objects of various weights and shapes and sizes, such as logs to build a fire or rocks to build a wall.
- Imagine lying in wet grass, silk sheets, or hot sand.
- Smell, touch, and study an imaginary rose.
- Touch, taste, and smell an imaginary lemon slice.
- Touch, taste, and smell an imaginary apple.
- Taste hot coffee, hot chocolate, hot tea. Taste cold soda, iced tea, cold lemonade.
- Remember the sound of a fingernail scraping against a blackboard or of a dentist's drill.

Exploring the following simple actions with imaginary objects improved finger and hand dexterity and the actor's sense of touch. As with all previous exercises, Moore required that actors choose circumstances to provide a context for the sense exploration.

- Nail a lid on a box.
- Peel a banana.
- Make a salad.
- Sew a button on a shirt.
- Make a bed.
- Sculpt a figure out of clay.

c. Exercises on the Floor

During every class, Sonia Moore and her teachers included exercises that compelled students to begin by lying on the floor. While using the floor for support, actors were able to work vigorously to pursue objectives and choose vivid gestures. The real, muscular effort required to confront the circumstances in these improvisations often completely absorbed, and sometimes exhausted, the actor physically and emotionally.

In these exercises students were forced to choose extreme circumstances within which to practice their skills. They were confronted with life-or-death situations and urged to struggle, physically and psychologically, to achieve objectives as they found themselves in, for example, car crashes, collapsed buildings, and quicksand. Battling obstacles was the crux of the activity as they worked to justify their choice of actions. Sonia Moore's goal here reflected Stanislavski's comments:

> It is a good thing in art when people are really alive, when they make an effort to reach a given point, when they repulse something, struggle for something . . . overcome obstacles or are even anguished. Battle brings victory and conquest. The worst is when all is quiescent in art, all in order . . . when there

is no need of argument, struggle, when there are no defeats, hence no victories either.[9]

- Imagine you have slipped and fallen into a muddy, smelly swamp. You struggle to move your limbs in the thick mud and make your way to dry ground.
- Imagine that the roof of your office building has collapsed and you find yourself pinned under debris. You struggle to free yourself as you find it difficult to breathe in the thick, dusty air.
- Imagine you have fallen on a frozen lake. As you struggle to get up in the bitter cold, you hear the ice cracking beneath you. Inch your way carefully to the edge of the lake.
- Imagine you are a diver on the bottom of the ocean floor searching for buried treasure. As you look for the treasure a shark approaches or your oxygen line gets caught in vegetation.
- Imagine you work in a glue factory. An explosion lands you on your back, covered, along with the floor and walls, in sticky glue. Struggle to stand up in the slippery mess and to escape the intoxicating smell.
- Imagine you and a close friend have lost control of a car and it has crashed. When you regain consciousness outside the vehicle, struggle to move your legs to reach your friend only to discover you are paralyzed.
- Imagine you find yourself stranded in a burning hot desert. Struggle with the sand, the heat, a windstorm, and thirst as you crawl your way to one oasis after another only to discover they are mirages.
- Imagine trespassing across a construction site. You accidentally slip into a vat of drying concrete. Struggle to remove your hands and feet as you avoid falling back into the concrete.

d. Silent Improvisations

In the early classes of each term, before they tackled scene work, students performed a variety of extended solo improvisations that gave them the opportunity to flesh out circumstances, physicalize their inner monologues with the steps of an action, and choose striking gestures. These improvisations were usually more fully developed and included the use of hand props and stage furniture.

- *Studying Late at Night.* You are up late studying for an exam. You hear a knock at the door. It startles you and you struggle to decide whether to answer it. A recent news bulletin has reported an escaped convict in the area, and the knock is frightening. You eventually make your way to the door only to discover that no one is there.
- *Argument.* You are in a deep sleep at home. You wake up to an explosive argument in the next room. The rising volume is frightening and you struggle to go back to sleep. You decide to do something about it

and cross to your bedroom door. Just as you touch the doorknob, the argument stops. Silence.

- *Lost Wallet.* You have dressed for a very important dinner meeting. As you grab your coat and check yourself in the mirror, you reach for your wallet. It is not where you normally leave it. Time is running out as you search everywhere for the wallet. Struggle to decide whether to stay and search or leave for the dinner.
- *Robbery.* You come home after a hard day at work. You enter your apartment and discover that your place has been ransacked and you have been robbed. After examining the objects that were carelessly tossed about and broken, you decide to call the police. With your hand on the receiver, you hear a noise in the next room. You struggle to decide what to do—investigate or rush out of the apartment.
- *Packing to Leave.* You have had a terrible fight with a roommate and decide to leave. As you pack a few things in your bedroom, you suddenly discover an object that makes you question your decision to leave. Struggle to decide what to do—stay or go.
- *Borrowing Money.* You are desperately and immediately in need of cash. You knock on your friend's door. No one is home but the door is open. As you enter you look around. You know she keeps a stash of emergency funds somewhere. You search everywhere. Finally, finding the wad of bills, you struggle whether or not to "borrow" the money.

e. Verbal Exercises

Occasionally, Sonia Moore would have students work on group exercises that were designed to create images in the minds of the listeners:

- Describe an accident in the street.
- Study the room and then, with eyes closed, describe it in detail.
- Describe the clothing of another class member.
- Describe the events of your day in minute detail.
- Describe a recent vacation.
- Defend your opinion of a favorite book or movie.
- Describe a piece of jewelry, a delicious dessert, or your pet.
- Relate a personal experience that was sad, exciting, or triumphant.

f. Varying Tempo-Rhythms of Exercises

All of the exercises described so far were often repeated in order to vary the tempo-rhythm of the activity. For example, students were directed to do the following:

- Justify walking, sitting down, or lying down in different tempo-rhythms.
- Pack a suitcase, wrap a gift, write a letter, get a glass of water in different tempos.

Or they were asked to work in two different tempo-rhythms simultaneously:

• You are angry at a friend's betrayal but attempt to be polite and cover up your feelings.
• You are ecstatic over good news but must remain solemn at an important meeting.

g. Structured Improvisation

Regardless of whether students were focused on solo, paired, or group exercises or exploring the actions and events of a scene, all work was pursued through the use of improvisation. Stanislavski discovered, as Sonia Moore did many years later, that an improvisation on an action or event provided a psychophysical experience for the actor. It created a set of circumstances that could not be duplicated by having the actors read and discuss the play. Improvisation led the actor through the process of transformation that resulted in Stanislavski's "reincarnation" with the character and the actor merging. The actor not only thinks and talks about the character's emotional and physical life, she actually lives it. As the actor absorbs the character, the character absorbs the actor, thus creating a new being.

The structured improvisations used by both Stanislavski in the last years of his life and Sonia Moore at her Studio required actors to make a series of decisions before starting. Actors needed to determine the circumstances of the situation, character relationships, the objective and obstacles confronting the character, the event of the improvisation, and the basic actions for the character to achieve the objective. Every improvisation needed a beginning, middle, and end. The example that follows demonstrates how improvisations were utilized in the Studio.

1. Improvisation on a Simple Physical Action

Sonia Moore often introduced students to the improvisational process by providing the background circumstances and encouraging them to fill in the blanks by making personal decisions that would flesh out the details of the exercise. The action for this exercise is "folding a sweater," and what follows is typical of how Moore would construct the improvisation.

Circumstances

Moore: You are packing to leave home to accept a new job. You've never lived on your own before, and now you will have an apartment by yourself. You are flying across the country and probably will not see your family for some time. The sweater is a parting gift from someone close to you.

Relationships

Moore: You love your family and are comfortable living at home. You will miss them terribly. The sweater reminds you of last night's good-bye dinner with them, and already you feel lonely.

Objective and obstacle

Moore: You feel torn because your objective is to prepare yourself for leaving, but your obstacle, your regret at the separation, makes you hesitate. You are thrilled at the prospect of a new job, but you are not anxious to leave friends and family behind.

Action

Moore: In order to achieve your objective, you struggle with your feelings and decide to finish packing by "folding a sweater."

Analogous emotion

Moore: Remember a time when you felt sad, even though it may have had nothing to do with packing to leave somewhere, and recall your behavior.

Event

Moore: You name this improvisation "Departure." Now you may begin.

As the actor began to work, she faced an open suitcase, holding the sweater in her hands. Throughout the exercise, Sonia Moore kept the student focused on the circumstances of the improvisation. Her verbal feedback, at times almost unobtrusive, at other times demanding, could prove to be a distraction. It took a while before students could incorporate her directions into their work. Eventually, her voice became a constant reminder to stay on course, meshing seamlessly with the actor's efforts.

Moore: Begin by moving the muscles of the torso while creating images of the people you are leaving. Wonder about all this and ask yourself questions. Can you survive on your own? What if you hate living alone? Keep moving the muscles as you evaluate your circumstances. You can take the job and leave, or stay and resign yourself to work that is not very inspiring. You make a decision that you need this job, even if leaving is difficult, and resolve to finish packing. You make a gesture that projects how you feel, your determination to go, and you fold the sweater. Now there is another gesture that reflects your feelings at having folded the sweater. Maybe satisfaction. Maybe regret. "Folding a sweater" is now a psychophysical action.

Though the preparation for the improvisation was structured, conscious work, Sonia Moore reminded students that the results were not. The spontaneous behavior that arose might trigger subconscious emotional or psychological reactions that were totally unpredictable but powerful and expressive. The goal of the improvisational work was to create a sequence of logical, believable, physical actions that were tied to the psychological life of the character.

II. MORE ADVANCED WORK

The complexity of the actors' work increased dramatically as they began to deal with a partner and undertake the complications of adding speech to improvisations. With paired improvisations, the focus was now on creating a sharp conflict and a clear superobjective and projecting an unambiguous relationship with a partner. Students gained practice choosing physical and verbal actions that were truthful, logical, and expressive. (Sonia Moore was fond of reminding actors that once they learned technique, they would spend the next twenty years learning how to make appropriate choices.) Finally, Moore emphasized the notion that speech arises out of necessity and needs to be treated as a precious commodity, "Words are the result of organic behavior. They flow after thoughts. Words are the crown of the process."[10] The transformation of the spoken word into verbal action is accomplished by using the same process—the inner monologue of steps accompanied by strong muscular work—which the actor used with physical action.

In preparation for vocal work, Sonia Moore and her teachers employed a variety of exercises to expand the actors' awareness of breathing, to relax the musculature of the face, particularly the mouth, and to strengthen articulation and projection. One of Moore's favorite assignments was the use of tongue twisters to improve articulation and, simultaneously, to provide practice with pursuing simple actions. For example, actors would use the tongue twister "Peter Piper Picked a Peck of Pickled Peppers" to attack, encourage, tease, or punish their partners who would, in turn, respond with appropriate counteractions. The lesson was always clear: the inherent meaning of the words changed with the addition of body gestures and vocal mechanics such as pitch, volume, and intonation. The actors concentrated on fulfilling actions rather than on the simple meaning of the words.

a. Sentence/Gestures

To reinforce the concept that gestures influence verbal actions, Moore used a "sentence/gesture" exercise. For example, actors would choose three sets of circumstances and objectives for a simple sentence such as:

- I'm going to the movies.
- Don't do that.
- I'm leaving.
- Please visit again soon.
- I won the lottery.

By working through the steps of an action (wondering, evaluating, and so forth) and choosing a gesture before and after the line for each set of circumstances, the meaning of the line shifted dramatically. Exercises such as this also encouraged students to explore large, expressive gestures that involved the entire body.

b. Group Work

1. Exercises in Communication

While solo exercises permitted students to work on technique, some group exercises forced them to concentrate on others' reactions and choices:

- In silence, move chairs into different configurations.
- Play musical chairs and sit quietly.
- Imagine sitting at a crowded airport, or attempt to observe one another without being noticed.
- Create a sculpture of victory or defeat, with each student joining in one at a time in a different pose. An earthquake causes it to crumble.
- The class creates a typewriter, with each student assigned a letter of the alphabet. A sentence is typed as each student claps for his letter. Everyone claps in between the words and at the end of a sentence.

2. Improvisations

Members of the Studio often worked as a unit, focusing on using the technique to account for other participants. Sonia Moore emphasized that actors needed to establish lines of honest, unbroken communication with each other on stage.[11] To reinforce that point, group improvisations required that the acting ensemble function as the following:

- Tightrope walkers auditioning for a job
- Thieves stealing a very heavy, priceless mirror from a museum
- Skiers caught in an avalanche trying to save each other
- Office workers stuck in an elevator at the end of a long, hard day
- Prisoners escaping by crawling under a fence
- Stranded travelers waiting for a plane that is delayed due to bad weather

- Defendants waiting in court for a verdict
- A family waiting in a doctor's office for a medical diagnosis

As a warm-up for partnered work, both nonverbal and verbal, Sonia Moore often employed the traditional "mirror exercise," which required actors to imitate not only each other's physical actions, but also each other's gestures.

c. Paired, Nonverbal Exercises

- *Bus Stop.* One character (*A*) waits for a bus on a dark, deserted street, anxious to return home to see to a sick friend. A second character (*B*) enters, having been stranded, penniless, in this part of town. *A* feels threatened and avoids *B*, who needs to borrow money from *A*. Each struggles to deal with the other. The improvisation ends when speech becomes necessary or the conflict is resolved.
- *Quarrel.* *A* and *B*, who have been living together for some time, have quarreled, and *A* decides to leave. As *A* packs, *B*, who regrets the argument, tries to apologize without speaking. *A* continues to avoid *B*. Each struggles to deal with the other's presence, and the exercise ends when speech becomes necessary or the conflict is resolved.

d. Paired, Verbal Exercises

- *Face-to-Face.* *A* and *B* face each other, *A* accusing *B*, and *B* defending herself. The circumstances can be built around the relationship; for example, *A* accuses *B* of being unfaithful, or attempting to "steal" *A*'s spouse. *B*, who decides whether to be guilty or innocent, defends her behavior, dress, and so on.
- *Airport Greeting.* Two friends meet at an airport for the first time in years. Separated by a crowd, they manage to find each other in the distance. Their only words are "Hello" accompanied by a physical greeting.
- *The Firing.* Actor *A* works for actor *B*. *A* comes to see *B* to ask for a raise while *B*, dissatisfied with *A*'s work, intends to fire him. They may like or dislike each other. (Conflicting feelings help to complicate the interaction.)
- *Sick Room.* *A* and *B* are relatives who have had a falling-out and no longer speak. *A* currently is nursing *C*, an offstage character who is gravely ill. *B* wants to visit *C* and *A* prevents that from happening through a verbal and physical struggle.
- *Borrower/Lender.* *A* is in trouble and needs to borrow money from *B*, whom she dislikes. *B* likes *A* but disapproves of the reason *A* needs the

money. The contradictions here can be communicated through gestures.

- *Separation.* *A* and *B* are parting, never to see each other again. *A* packs to leave, and *B* prepares a final meal. Because the tension is so thick, they speak about the weather instead of what is really on their minds.
- *Telephone Conversation.* Carry on a phone conversation using only "Yes" or "No." Treat the conversation as dialogue, communicating attitudes and feelings through physical behavior.
- *Improvisations on Strong Actions.* Two actors each choose a vivid action and create a scene around their choices by supplying circumstances, objectives, and obstacles. Strong examples of actions are mocking, embarrassing, seducing, humiliating, threatening, competing, pleading, blackmailing, and rejecting. The more conflict created by the choices, the more substantial the improvisation.
- *Two Actions.* Two actors create a scene around two unrelated physical actions. For example, one actor might pound the floor while the other crosses to a window. They justify the actions by supplying circumstances and objectives.
- *Spies and Detectives.* Two spies meet at a train station or airport to pass a message from one to the other. A detective appears and attempts to intercept the message. None of the actors knows who plays what role.

All of the above exercises require added detail and specific circumstances, objectives, and obstacles. They also provide the opportunity for actors to practice psychophysical involvement by using the steps of an action as an inner monologue that accompanies the work with the muscles.

III. SCENE STUDY

a. Group Work: *The Three Sisters*

Sonia Moore used Chekhov's *The Three Sisters* to initiate new members of the Studio to scene work. Students performed either an Olga or an Andrei monologue. After a brief discussion of the circumstances of the play and the scene, and a completed character biography written by the actor, Moore went to work.[12] She rehearsed each student, drilling them in the nonverbal specifics of the moment preceding the scene and in the choice of appropriate gestures to express the character's inner state. Work on *The Three Sisters* was, for the most part, dictated by Sonia Moore and carried out by the actor. There was no improvisational exploration of the character's life or the circumstances of the play, as there would be later when students undertook the study of their own individual characters and scenes. *The Three Sisters* was simply an opportunity for each actor to begin the process of examining a character's words and incorporating Moore's steps of an action (the inner monologue) with Olga's or Andrei's external monologue.

b. Individual Work on a Character

Students were usually assigned their first scenes by Sonia Moore from a list of plays that she frequently used for class. Most were modern American and European classics by playwrights such as Edward Albee, Eugene O'Neill, Arthur Miller, Lillian Hellman, Anton Chekhov, and August Strindberg and featured clearly defined characters with vivid, emotionally involving actions. Scenes were well balanced, providing equal stage time for each partner, and presented the actors with two worthy adversaries. The conflict of the scene was, most often, powerful and challenging.

1. Preliminary Analysis

The initial analysis of the play and character required that the actor do the following:

- Read the play several times for a detailed understanding of its circumstances (who, what, when, where, and why) and the through line of actions and events.
- Write a character biography in the first person, filling in the gaps left by the playwright and exploring the character's life before the play begins.
- Determine the character's superobjective (the overriding want that controls the character's behavior throughout the play) and scene objective.
- Determine the spine of the play (the playwright's intent).
- Provide a noun name for the scene; that is, a one- or two-word title that summarizes the action of the scene.

2. Character Improvisations

At this point, Sonia Moore directed students to begin the series of improvisations used to explore (1) the character's background and (2) the events of the scene. With the written biography as a source, improvisations were created around a single event, relationship, or physical action in the character's life. The focus was on behavioral choices, not dialogue, and the intent of the improvisation was to reveal significant actions that would prompt emotional responses. This period of investigation could last weeks, or months, before the actors were permitted to turn to the script and might include these improvisations:

- Interactions with family members and significant friends that occurred earlier in the character's life.
- The first meeting between characters.
- Significant events between characters that might have occurred before the play begins.
- Offstage moments that actually occur in the course of the play and are referred to in the script, though never seen.
- Primary events of the play that affect the characters' lives and objectives.

Once the play and the characters had been explored in detail, Sonia Moore would lead students through a series of improvisations on the scene itself. For example, actors physically analyzed the moment before the scene began as well as the primary actions of the scene, as though each action were a miniscene in itself.

3. Improvisation on an Event from a Play

By actually living through events or moments in a play, students at the Studio shaped the life of the character in a concrete, personal fashion, as did Stanislavski's actors when rehearsing *Tartuffe* in 1938. The following was a typical improvisation from Arthur Miller's *The Crucible*, a play Sonia Moore loved and used repeatedly in classes through the years. In it, the actors playing Elizabeth Proctor and Abigail Williams explore their relationship by recreating the scene, referred to in the play, when Elizabeth sends Abigail away following Abigail's explosive affair with John Proctor. In this example, the focus is on Elizabeth.

Circumstances

Moore: Elizabeth, you are married to John Proctor. You live in Salem, Massachusetts, in 1672 and have three children. During your last pregnancy you became very ill and your husband John hired a young girl, Abigail, to help with the children and the housework. You are a religious, somewhat self-righteous woman and after discovering John's adultery are determined to "put Abigail out."

Relationships

Moore: You still love John, though you have not completely forgiven him. You don't know if you can trust him anymore. As a Christian woman, you should not hate anyone, but you despise what Abigail has done and the sight of her stirs feelings of anger and jealousy.

Objective and obstacle

Moore: Though you know your decision is right, you are torn because your objective is to remove this evil from your lives, and this temptation from John's eyes, but you face obstacles. You wish to act with charity, but you are disturbed that John himself is not putting Abigail out. You want Abigail gone, but you do not want to look her in the face.

Actions

Moore: In order to achieve your objective, you confront Abigail first thing this morning, demand that she pack her things, prevent her from lying or defending herself, and give her a week's wages because it would be the charitable thing to do.

Analogous emotion

Moore: Remember a time when you were tormented with jealousy and hurt. You are angry! Search your emotional memory for a time when you felt the same feelings, not the same situation, and recall your physical behavior.

Event

Moore: We will call the event of this improvisation "Confrontation." Now you are ready to begin.

The structure of the improvisations at the Studio was very specific. Though every detail was not predetermined by the actors, the background circumstances, general direction, and basic events were apparent. With this much preparation, physical and verbal actions arose spontaneously and often evoked unusual, fascinating reactions from the actors. Moore takes the actor playing Elizabeth through the initial moment.

Moore: You have done the conscious work. Now let your subconscious take over. If you are comfortable in the circumstances, you are not wasting time trying to think of something to do. Elizabeth, you are standing at the kitchen table. Begin to move your muscles as you wonder what you will say when Abigail appears. Evaluate your circumstances and your desire to put her out and struggle to make a decision about your first words to her. You feel Abigail enter the kitchen behind you. There is a subtle gesture, a small physical adjustment and then the verbal action: "Abigail!" Another gesture, perhaps expressing your pain and anger, follows.

c. Table Work

The extensive period of improvisation on the characters' lives and the actions of the scene was followed by reading and discussing the text while "sitting around the table." While working through the script, Sonia Moore pushed students to play verbal actions as fully as possible; that is, to wonder, evaluate, make a decision, and execute a gesture before and after each line of speech. The gestures were often subtle and primarily involved the upper body. Sonia Moore viewed table work as an opportunity to transform the actor's speech into verbal action and to encourage the actor to begin communicating with her partner in a meaningful way.

IV. PREPRODUCTION WORK: A VIEW FROM THE BRIDGE

Members of the Studio performed improvisations both in rehearsal and in the classroom until they "could do anything as the character." That is, until they could live comfortably in the character's shoes. What follows is a demonstration of the use of the Method of Physical Actions as it is applied to Arthur Miller's *A View from the Bridge*. This play met the basic criterion for production advocated by both Stanislavski and Sonia Moore: a play must contain important ideas and conflicts and deserve to be embodied on the stage.

In *A View from the Bridge*, Arthur Miller's characters grapple with right and wrong, with difficult relationships and failed dreams, and with moral dilemmas and secrets that must be kept hidden. The subtext of thoughts and feelings, often in conflict with the text, make it an ideal choice with which to practice Moore's inner monologue/steps of an action and to explore gestures to project the actor's inner state.

a. Preliminary Play Analysis

Multiple readings of the script reveal the details of the given circumstances, the characters and their objectives, and the main idea, or spine, of the play. Before improvisations began, Sonia Moore insisted that students complete this preliminary analysis.

Given Circumstances

A View from the Bridge takes place in the Red Hook section of Brooklyn in the early 1950s. Its characters are struggling to live and work in somewhat meager circumstances. Eddie, the head of the Carbone family, supports his wife and niece by working on the New York piers as regularly as possible. The play emphasizes the importance of family ties and the lengths to which individuals will go to protect those ties. Money may be scarce but family still comes first. At the same time, a current of irrational fear of the unknown and a desperate need to hide behind what is understood and familiar run through the play. These circumstances present fertile ground in which the seeds of mistrust, paranoia, and jealousy may be sown and flourish.

Primary characters

- Eddie Carbone, a man of about forty, has spent most of his adult life on the docks. He is devoted to his family, and Catherine, his niece, is the center of his life. He cannot bear to see her growing up and, therefore, will not let go. Eddie cannot acknowledge his deep-seated feelings about Catherine.
- Beatrice, Eddie's wife, a woman in her late thirties, is a homemaker who spends her time making life in their sparse environment comfortable. She is kind and big-hearted—she offers their home to visiting cousins— and loves Eddie and Catherine. But lately she's begun to notice a change in Eddie. She realizes he is too attached to Catherine.
- Catherine, their niece, the daughter of Beatrice's dead sister, is seventeen, pretty, and on the brink of womanhood. Catherine loves Beatrice but has formed a very special relationship with Eddie. They are unusually close. As a grown woman, she wants to test her wings, but Eddie is afraid to let her go.
- Marco, Beatrice's cousin, comes to America to escape the poverty in Italy and to find work to support his family back home. He is in his early thirties and is the strong, silent type. Marco loves his younger brother, Rodolpho, and doesn't understand Eddie's distrust of him.
- Rodolpho, Marco's brother in his mid-twenties, is enamored of the American way of life and of Catherine. Playful and flamboyant, he spends what he makes working on the docks on clothes and records, and he likes to sing, cook, and sew. He and Catherine are in love and contemplating marriage. Rodolpho never understands the extent of Eddie's rage.
- Alfieri is a neighborhood lawyer in his fifties. Gentle, good-humored, and thoughtful, he is committed to his practice among the longshoremen and their families of Red Hook, Brooklyn. Eddie seeks Alfieri's legal advice in order to prevent Catherine's marriage to Rodolpho.

Spine of the play   Miller's controlling idea—that by denying basic truths about ourselves we ultimately destroy ourselves—governs all events and actions of the play and provides its shape. In *A View from the Bridge*, the inability to face personal and social truths results in catastrophic, tragic events. Eddie's obsession with Catherine began with a genuine and appropriate love for his niece. However, when he should have let her go and permitted nature to take its course, he could not confront feelings that were so deep-seated and unmentionable that he would have to die to protect them.

His tragedy was marked by his fatal flaw—an inability to see himself, Catherine, Beatrice, Rodolpho, and Marco clearly.

b. Improvisations on Events of the Play

The active analysis of the play begins with improvisations on events and actions. Sonia Moore was quick to remind actors at the Studio that the Method of Physical Actions required physical work. She regularly warned students not to let the improvisation bog down in "conversation."

These sample improvisations might be used to explore events involving Eddie, Beatrice, and Catherine before the play begins. Notice that each improvisation has a title.

- *The Provider.* Catherine is sick, money is tight, and Eddie cannot find work. Beatrice scrimps but Eddie is haunted by his promise to Catherine's mother.
- *A Threesome.* Beatrice and Eddie plan a day out together, their first time in months. Catherine, twelve or thirteen, throws a tantrum and wants to be included.
- *The Dance.* Catherine, now in high school, is invited to her first big dance. Eddie does not want her to go and argues with Beatrice.
- *Secretarial School.* Catherine is graduating from high school. Eddie wants her to enroll in secretarial school, but Catherine and Beatrice want her to take a job she has been offered.
- *The Letter.* Beatrice receives a letter from her cousins in Italy in which they inform her that they plan to come to America to find work.

The moment just before the play begins might be explored with this improvisation:

- *The Rehearsal.* Beatrice and Catherine prepare a plan of attack to present Eddie with Catherine's new job opportunity.

Events within the play that occur offstage, generally between scenes, might be explored in these improvisations:

- *Employment.* Eddie, Marco, and Rodolpho set off for the cousins' first morning of work. Eddie notices Rodolpho and Catherine with their heads together.
- *The Visit.* Beatrice visits her mother and tries to hide the growing problems with Eddie.
- *The Date.* Catherine and Rodolpho head out on their first date. Everyone but Eddie is happy.

- *The Rebuff.* Beatrice tries to touch Eddie. He rejects her when Catherine enters the room.
- *Eavesdropping.* Beatrice watches Catherine sitting on the edge of the bathtub talking to Eddie while he shaves. They do not see her.

Sonia Moore suggested that these improvisations should be brief, simple, and to the point. Physical actions were chosen to achieve the objective of the exercise, and dialogue was inserted only when necessary. By performing a series of improvisations, actors were gradually, but actively, analyzing the play and characters.

c. Character Improvisations

Shifting focus from the play as a whole to a particular character and scene demanded that the actor write the character's biography. It included information on family relationships, childhood experiences of importance, lifestyle, dreams and fears, first contact with the partner's character (if it occurred before the scene), and any other events outside the play that influenced the character's behavior.

For Beatrice, the character biography might establish her relationship with her dead sister; create a beginning for her relationship with Eddie; explain how Eddie and Beatrice became Catherine's parents; and clarify her current issues with Eddie and Catherine. Beatrice's superobjective is to preserve her marriage, her family, and the stability of her home life. She sees problems brewing and attempts to steer clear of them and keep Eddie focused on their marriage. Beatrice is only too aware of Eddie's denial and senses that the final confrontation is coming. Afraid of Eddie's feelings for Catherine, and of the conflict between Eddie and Rodolpho, Beatrice urges Eddie to face reality and give up Catherine.

Character improvisations are suggested by the biography. For Beatrice, the actor could explore:

- Beatrice and her sister at home as teenagers
- Beatrice's first meeting with Eddie
- Eddie's proposal to Beatrice
- Beatrice and Eddie early in their marriage, happy and having fun
- Beatrice and Eddie taking Catherine home with them
- Beatrice watching Eddie and Catherine together and experiencing the first pangs of jealousy
- Beatrice discovering Eddie waiting up for Catherine to come home from a party and seeing the first hints of his obsession
- Beatrice and Catherine competing for Eddie's attention

All of these improvisations serve to expand the actor's physical and psychological sense of the character. This period of the rehearsal process, whether for a scene or an entire play, lasted until Sonia Moore decided that the students had a firm grasp on the details of the role.

d. Improvisations on the Actions of a Scene

The analysis of an individual scene began with a clear understanding of the actions of the scene and the objectives of the characters. In Act I, Scene 2, a few weeks after the arrival of the cousins from Italy, Eddie is brooding outside on the front steps, waiting for Catherine and Rodolpho to come home from a date. He is convinced that Rodolpho intends to take advantage of Catherine and that he is about to lose her. Beatrice arrives home from an evening out. Eddie wants to wait outside until Catherine is home safe and then confront her with his fears about Rodolpho. Beatrice wants to get Eddie to give up his vigil, forget his obsession with Rodolpho, and face the possibility of Catherine's marriage to Rodolpho. This scene is titled "Trouble Brewing."

Actively analyzing the scene could include these improvisations on offstage moments before the scene:

- Catherine and Roldolpho getting dressed for their date while Eddie tries to distract Catherine
- Rodolpho earlier in the day singing on board ship, unaware that the other longshoremen are mocking him
- Beatrice attempting to create an intimate moment with Eddie and failing

Improvisations on the primary actions of this scene can be performed both in and out of the circumstances of the scene. For example:

- Eddie attacking Rodolpho
- Beatrice defending Catherine and Rodolpho
- Beatrice teasing Eddie and suggesting he is jealous
- Beatrice confronting Eddie on their lack of intimacy
- Eddie blaming the arrival of the cousins for his lack of interest
- Beatrice warning Eddie to let Catherine go

Discovering what impact these core actions have on the characters and the scene is enhanced when the moments are investigated away from the situation of the scene. For example, "Eddie attacking Rodolpho" can be played with the family at home, at work, with or without Catherine, or in a restaurant. The actors are not duplicating the scene, necessarily, but analyzing the action physically and emotionally. When actors return to the scene, their understanding of the action is augmented by having lived it in other circumstances.

V. SAMPLE CLASSES

Here are two sample classes from the Sonia Moore Studio intended to provide a feel for the structure of individual sessions. Both include warm-up activities as well as exercises that give students the opportunity to develop technique. The beginning class is a model for actors in the initial phase of their study and covers an introduction to approaching character in *The Three Sisters*. The more advanced class, while still offering work on technique through a variety of individual and group assignments, focuses on scene study as students pursue the analysis and performance of characters in suggested plays. (In each category of exercise, two are presented, from which one or both may be chosen for inclusion in any one class. Though more are suggested than may be covered in a two-hour class, the groupings provide various options for the teacher. The numbering refers to the fuller list of exercises for that category included earlier in the chapter.) Each of these exercises and improvisations would incorporate the steps of an action and encourage students to explore the body's muscles.

BEGINNING CLASS

Warm-up: Relaxation (I.a.1.)

- Imagine yourself to be a marionette with strings attached at the back of your head, shoulders, hips, and knees. Cut the strings one by one, releasing the body until you gradually collapse, like a puppet, to the floor.
- While lying on the floor, imagine your body is a balloon filled with sand. A series of zippers throughout the body (for example, from fingertips to shoulder) keep the sand inside. Release each zipper and feel body tension flow out with the sand.

Simple Actions in Various Circumstances (I.b.1.)

- Look through a pair of binoculars.
- Open or close a window or door.

Using Sense Memory (I.b.2.)

- Remember the sound of a fingernail scraping against a blackboard or a dentist's drill.
- Make a bed.

Exercises on the Floor (I.c.)

- Imagine you have fallen on a frozen lake. As you struggle to get up in the bitter cold, you hear the ice cracking beneath you. Inch your way carefully to the edge of the lake.
- Imagine you are a diver on the bottom of the ocean floor searching for buried treasure. As you look for the treasure a shark approaches or your oxygen line gets caught in vegetation.

Group Work: Exercises on Communication (II.b.1.)

- Create a sculpture of victory or defeat. Each student joins in one at a time in a different pose. An earthquake causes the completed sculpture to crumble.
- The class creates a typewriter and each student is assigned a letter of the alphabet. A sentence is typed as each student claps for his letter. Everyone claps in between the words and at the end of a sentence.

Solo, Nonverbal Improvisations (I.d.)

- *Lost Wallet.* You have dressed for a very important dinner meeting. As you grab your coat and check yourself in the mirror, you look for your wallet. It is not where you normally leave it. Time is running out as you search everywhere for the wallet. Struggle to decide whether to stay and search or leave for the dinner.
- *Studying Late at Night.* You are up late studying for an exam. You hear a knock at the door. It startles you and you struggle to decide whether to answer it. A recent news bulletin has reported an escaped convict in the area and the knock is frightening. You eventually make your way to the door only to discover that no one is there.

Work on *The Three Sisters*: Olga's opening monologue (III.a.)

- After you have read the entire play and created a biography for Olga from the first-person point of view, prior to the beginning of the play, the monologue is worked on in class.

- Olga's objective is to encourage Irina, who sits in the same room as her sister. Choose actions to achieve this objective.
- Have some idea of what the character is thinking and feeling when not speaking (inner monologue). Example: Olga is marking papers in a rush to get ready for Irina's celebration. The clock chimes, and she remembers the same day a year ago. She compares this day with the past one, astonished at the difference, "Father died a year ago today, Irina. Your Saint's Day. It was cold and snowing. I thought I should never live through it. . . ."
- Make physical choices through the steps of wondering, evaluating, and deciding.
- Choose gestures to project what you are thinking and feeling.

ADVANCED CLASS

Warm-up: Relaxation of Muscles (I.a.1.)

- While lying on the floor, progressively tense and relax all muscles groups from the feet to the top of the head, taking an inventory of places where you hold tension.
- An alternate method of relaxation is to focus attention on an object, remaining in the here and now. Lie on the floor, eyes open. Focus overhead on the ceiling and describe aloud whatever is seen, continuously, for five minutes.

Simple Actions in Various Circumstances (I.b.1.)

- Walk the floor to quiet the noisy neighbors downstairs. Walk the floor to kill a bug.
- Hang a picture on a wall that was a gift from a friend. Hang a picture on a wall that you are obligated to keep.

or

Using Sense Memory (I.b.2.)

- Imagine the smell and feel of wet wool.
- Imagine lying in wet grass, silk sheets, or hot sand.

Exercises on the Floor (I.c.)

- Imagine you and a close friend have lost control of a car and it has crashed. When you regain consciousness outside the vehicle, struggle

to move your legs to reach your friend only to discover you are paralyzed.
- Imagine trespassing across a construction site. You accidentally slip into a vat of drying concrete. Struggle to remove your hands and feet as you avoid falling back into the concrete.

or

Silent Improvisations (I.d.)

- *Robbery.* You come home after a hard day at work. You enter your apartment and discover your place has been ransacked and you have been robbed. After examining the objects that were carelessly tossed about and broken, you decide to call the police. With your hand on the receiver, you hear a noise in the next room. You struggle to decide what to do—investigate or rush out of the apartment.
- *Packing to Leave.* You have had a terrible fight with a roommate and decide to leave. As you pack a few things in your bedroom, you suddenly discover an object that makes you question your decision to leave. Struggle to decide what to do—stay or go.

Varying Tempo-Rhythms of Exercises (I.f.)

Working in two different tempo-rhythms simultaneously:

- You are angry at a friend's betrayal but attempt to be polite and cover up your feelings.
- You are ecstatic over good news but must remain solemn at an important meeting.

or

Group Improvisations (II.b.2.)

- Tightrope walkers auditioning for a job
- Office workers stuck in an elevator at the end of a long, hard day

Paired, Verbal Exercises (II.d.)

- *Sick Room.* A and B are relatives who have had a falling-out and no longer speak. A currently is nursing C, an offstage character who is gravely ill. B wants to visit C and A prevents that from happening through a verbal and physical struggle.

- *Improvisations on Strong Actions.* Two actors each choose a vivid action and create a scene around their choices by supplying circumstances, objectives, and obstacles. Strong examples of actions are mocking, embarrassing, flirting, humiliating, threatening, competing, pleading, blackmailing, and rejecting. The more conflict created by the choices, the more substantial the improvisation.

Character Improvisations

After preliminary scene analysis (III.b.1.), students begin improvisations on actions and events in and around the play (III.b.2., 3.):

- The first meeting between characters
- Significant events between characters that might have occurred before the play begins

or

Rehearsal of the Scene

After a significant period of improvisation, students begin to rehearse the scene using the playwright's text and improvising staging in a defined setting.

Sonia Moore's use of the Method of Physical Actions provided a unique insight into the events of a play. Rather than simply *knowing* the action, actors actually *lived* the action. As they moved from an active analysis of the play to the rehearsal of the text, they meshed physical actions discovered during improvisations with the verbal actions of the script. Even while rehearsing scenes, Moore would occasionally return to improvisations to keep character relationships fresh.

NOTES

1. Many students stayed beyond the two-year period, even those who had been awarded certificates. Sonia Moore offered some of these students full scholarships to continue to study.

2. This curriculum was listed in the National Association of Schools of Theatre (NAST) Self-Study, written in 1991 in preparation for the NAST visitation in spring 1992. The reaccreditation actually took place in spring 1993.

3. Moore's early years at the Third Studio left an indelible impression on her regarding discipline. She had high expectations pertaining to student behavior and commitment to the Studio. Even in her last years she would chastise actors about their

work ethic, urge them to keep the space clean, and generally lecture them on appropriate conduct while they were attending the Sonia Moore Studio.

4. Though in theory students were cast in productions after several terms of study, members were sometimes cast earlier, depending on demonstrated acting skill. Conversely, pupils were not automatically cast in a production during their fourth term.

5. *The Sonia Moore Studio of the Theatre Student Handbook* (New York: American Center for Stanislavski Theatre Art, n.d.), 17–19, collection of Elizabeth C. Stroppel.

6. Mel Gordon, *The Stanislavsky Technique* (New York: Applause Theatre Book Publishers, 1987), 105, 107.

7. These exercises are from a list distributed to teachers at the Studio during the 1970s and early 1980s.

8. Sonia Moore, *Stanislavski Revealed: The Solution to Spontaneity on Stage* (New York: Applause Theatre Books, 1991), 179.

9. Constantin Stanislavski, *Stanislavski's Legacy*, ed. and trans. Elizabeth Reynolds Hapgood (New York: Theatre Arts Books, 1958), 29.

10. Sonia Moore as recorded in the class notes from the collection of Elizabeth C. Stroppel.

11. Moore, *Stanislavski Revealed*, 187.

12. In *Training an Actor*, Moore included sample biographies for the characters of Olga and Andrei.

Conclusion

Sonia Moore enjoyed a larger-than-life existence. It is no wonder, then, that the superobjective of her career was equally outsized. She wanted nothing less than to transform the American theatre. Through her books, her Studio, and her tenacious loyalty to his work, Moore kept Stanislavski's System—as distinct from the American Method—front and center in the American theatre psyche.

Nevertheless, questions remain. Why did the Studio deteriorate in its last years and close its doors at her death? Why have so few actors who studied at the Studio achieved prominence? Why has Sonia Moore not occupied a position of importance similar to other great acting teachers of the twentieth century?

Her Russian orientation to Stanislavski's work made her somewhat of an outsider. She shared the stage in the New York acting scene with Strasberg, Lewis, and Adler, but, unlike them, her background did not include learning Stanislavski during the fermentation of the Group Theatre years. Instead, in 1957 Sonia Moore materialized already formed. Though she found tremendous success with her books, Moore could not, ultimately, duplicate the same level of triumph with her Studio that other prominent acting figures achieved with theirs.

As she reached her ninth decade of life and the Studio its fourth, the degree to which the Studio depended on Moore's personal finances for its existence became all too obvious. By this time, the number of students also had declined, making the operation extraordinarily cost inefficient. And yet, it was painfully obvious that the Studio could not die while Sonia Moore lived. Her work had been a central focus of her life for so many years that surrendering to finances and low enrollment seemed out of the question. She kept hoping, even to the end, that sufficient funding would appear in order to extend the Studio's existence into the future. But because she *was* the Studio, it is doubtful that, even had funding been granted, it could have survived the absence of Sonia Moore's presence.

There were, however, other factors that contributed to the closing of the Studio. Moore's need to control all facets of the organization resulted in paradoxical behavior that threatened the survival of the Studio and, on occasion, drove students and teachers away. Though she wanted her students to "spread the word" about Stanislavski, she also clung to many of them, demanding that they remain with her because they "did not know enough." From time to time she permitted one student or another to assume a degree of responsibility in the affairs of the Studio. She never, however, appointed artistic leadership strong enough to take the reins should she be unable to do so. Her offer to Anatoly Smeliansky to serve as artistic director in the 1990s was a ceremonial gesture, occurring too late in the Studio's life to have any real impact.

The production schedule maintained during earlier decades was an indication of the health and prosperity of the Studio. When enrollment decreased, a reduction in the number of shows occurred. While fewer plays were presented during the late 1980s and 1990s, Sonia Moore's research and writing continued to thrive, and her involvement with the academic community intensified. By this time, she had expanded Stanislavski's Method of Physical Actions to incorporate her own technique, which became more important than the production of plays.

In the 1970s and early 1980s, when she worked primarily with Stanislavski's version of the Method of Physical Actions, actively analyzing the character and play via improvisations, with less focus on the muscles, her work was noticeably easier to realize. Because of her additions, some teachers at the Studio chose to create their own interpretations of her process in an effort to make it more accessible. In the end, it is impossible to know how many students, artists, and academics truly comprehended her version of the Method of Physical Actions or believed in its practicality.

Sonia Moore's adaptation could be remarkable for enhancing actors' concentration on character work, but it generated skepticism. (A theatre practitioner once commented that he could not imagine a certain television star worrying about which muscle to move.) Too often, putting the spotlight on muscles forced actors to focus on themselves and limited the attention paid to other performers sharing the stage. Many of the students at the Studio were young and inexperienced, and had no sense of themselves as actors or how to mesh her process with their own emotional lives. Given the regimen of the Studio, an actor's personal connection to a character was not a priority and took a back seat to the exploration of her technique.

Another question demands an answer. Why have so few of her former students attained prominence as actors? Though a variety of answers may be found, the most significant one may not be the most obvious: the priorities Sonia Moore established for her Studio. She valued teaching more than she valued performing. It was her belief that the Method of Physical Actions, and her refinement of it, could be spread more efficiently by having it taught rather than by having it performed. She initiated a pattern in the 1960s that continued to the closing days of the Studio: when certain students could demonstrate competence as actors, as well as an intellectual curiosity about acting, she invited them to become teachers. The majority of the acting faculty who were listed in the Studio brochures from the 1960s through the 1990s were former students. For Sonia Moore, transforming the American theatre would come as a result of training teachers in the Stanislavski System.

Many actors learned about her through her books, and she aligned herself with professional organizations that were primarily academic in nature. Moore also found in this arena a legitimacy she never fully acquired in the world of professional theatre. At conferences and workshops she occupied a place of significance whether she was lecturing on Stanislavski's legacy, demonstrating her work with the steps and muscles, or sharing excerpts from her memoir. For Moore the importance of the process far outweighed the value of the product. Other prominent acting studios make their famous alumni the cornerstone of their recruitment efforts, which, in turn, contributes to their financial health and supports the future of the institutions. This was not possible with the Sonia Moore Studio.

A final question remains. Why has Sonia Moore not occupied a position of prominence similar to other great acting teachers of the twentieth century? The answer probably lies in several of the issues already described. Her critical attitude toward other acting teachers, studios, and styles of American acting training minimized her popularity among her peers. Though she may have lacked the fame enjoyed by the heads of other New York studios, she was greatly respected and admired around the country. For the teachers and students who did not know her personally, her books became a way of meeting Sonia Moore and provided her with a position of authority. Her work continues to live on in all of those individuals influenced by their time at the Studio. The authors themselves still use what they learned and taught at the Studio.

The Sonia Moore Studio of the Theatre may have been the only studio publicly dedicated to using the Method of Physical Actions as a way of exploring text and stirring the actor's emotional life. Information on Stanislavski's System began trickling into this country with the arrival of the MAT in the 1920s and with the publication of his books, and other texts about his working process, beginning in the 1930s. As suggested by her bibliographies, Sonia Moore, however, made a point of avoiding English translations of Russian materials, including the English versions of Stanislavski's three texts.[1] Neither does she refer to other books on Stanislavski, written in English by theatre scholars and artists, although material was available.

In 1973 Moore replied to an article in *TDR* by Jack Poggi, and her letter suggests that she was familiar with some American scholarship and was aware that Americans were visiting Russia and studying Stanislavski's System in practice. Nevertheless, she is emphatic in her letter to the editor in reaction to what she perceives as Poggi's oversimplification of Stanislavski's theories. She asserts that Stanislavski's importance has never been fully understood in America. "That Stanislavski . . . finally found the answer to his quest of four decades is completely unknown in this country."[2] On the contrary, some Americans did appear to have known about Stanislavski's exploration with action. What seemed to be missing, with the exception of work at the Sonia Moore Studio, was the practical experimentation with Stanislavski's legacy.

In recent years books have emerged describing Stanislavski's discoveries in theory and practice—most published after her death in 1995. For example, Jean Benedetti in *Stanislavski and the Actor* (1998) tackles the application of the Method of Physical Actions to the classroom and the rehearsal process. The author acknowledges the difficulty of grasping the System from Stanislavski's books—from editing and translating problems through Stanislavski's awkward terminology and the fragmentary nature of his writings. He asks, how are teachers and students of acting to study the System? His response is found in the personal notes taken by Irina Novitskaya, one of Stanislavski's assistants at the Opera-Dramatic Studio, who transformed her record of events at the Studio into her book *Uroki Vdoxnovenija* (*Inspiring Lessons*) (1984). Supplemented by Benedetti's own research and experience with Stanislavski's System, and utilizing an updated vocabulary, *Uroki Vdoxnovenija* provides the core of *Stanislavski and the Actor*.[3] Benedetti's rationale for his "modernisation" of Stanislavski's work mirrored Sonia Moore's explanation for the creation of her technique: Stanislavski insisted that his work should be useful and "that it should be extended and developed."[4]

The exercises and improvisations take the actor through the elements of Stanislavski's System and an explanation and demonstration of the Method of Physical Actions. Benedetti's sample breakdown of the play into episodes and events for analysis through improvisation parallels Stanislavski's description of the phases of rehearsal. It is a contemporary, practical application, and it echoes much of the work explored at the Sonia Moore Studio from the 1960s to the 1990s. Moore taught the same process Stanislavski outlined in the late 1930s, now summarized by Benedetti.

Two books by British actor and scholar Bella Merlin, *Beyond Stanislavsky* (2001) and *Konstantin Stanislavsky* (2003), describe further the use of his final experiments with physical action. *Beyond Stanislavsky* chronicles Merlin's ten-month participation in an actor-training program at Moscow's State Institute of Cinematography in 1993 and 1994. She was led through a "hands-on training in the integrative approach to acting proposed by Stanislavsky,"[5] designed to guide actors through a process of working on the self, the ensemble, and the role. She offers a fascinating glimpse into contemporary Russian teaching and rehearsal processes that begin with Stanislavski's System and move beyond it to encompass the work of Chekhov, Grotowski, and others. Nevertheless, the emphasis is on an improvisational approach to acting that references Stanislavski's final exploration with action. *Konstantin Stanislavsky* supplies exercises on the utilization of the Method of Physical Actions and active analysis for the classroom and rehearsal studio. Some of the activities and improvisations resemble those included in the program of study at the Sonia Moore Studio.[6] It is likely that these books represent merely the tip of the acting iceberg: more work on these processes will, no doubt, appear in future scholarship and practice as additional information from Stanislavski's life and work becomes available.

History will judge the extent of Sonia Moore's contribution to American acting training. But for those of us touched by her presence, there is only one way to respond to Moore's efforts to repay her debt to her adopted country: paid in full.

NOTES

1. Gray reports that as early as 1930, Stanislavski wrote a "Directing and Acting" entry for the *Encyclopaedia Britannica*. It included sections on breaking down a role into its segments and building a character by creating an unbroken line of action. Both notions suggest Stanislavski was referring to his initial work with the Method of Physical Actions. Paul Gray, "Stanislavski and America: A Critical Chronology," in "Stanislavski and America: 2," ed. Richard Schechner, special issue, *TDR* 9, no. 2 (Winter 1964): 31–32.

2. Sonia Moore, "A Reaction to T-57 Article on Stanislavsky," *TDR* 17, no. 2 (June 1973): 136; Jack Poggi, "The Stanislavsky System in Russia," *TDR* 17, no. 1 (March 1973): 124–33.

3. Jean Benedetti, *Stanislavski and the Actor* (New York: Routledge / Theatre Arts Books, 1998), vii–xv.

4. Benedetti, *Stanislavski and the Actor*, xiv.

5. Bella Merlin, *Beyond Stanislavsky* (New York: Routledge / Theatre Arts Books, 2001), 5.

6. Bella Merlin, *Konstantin Stanislavsky* (New York: Routledge, 2003).

Selected Bibliography

American Center for Stanislavski Theatre Art Papers, New York Public Library for the Performing Arts.

American Stanislavski Theatre Papers, New York Public Library for the Performing Arts.

Benedetti, Jean. *Stanislavski: A Biography*. New York: Routledge, 1988.

———. *Stanislavski and the Actor*. New York: Routledge / Theatre Arts Books, 1998.

Bennett, Phillip G. Interview by the authors. Tape recording. June 25 and July 2, 2002.

Black, Lendley C. *Michael Chekhov as Actor, Director and Teacher*. Ann Arbor: UMI Research Press, 1987.

Bloch, Susana, Pedro Orthous, and Guy Santibañez-H. "Effector Patterns of Basic Emotions: A Psychophysiological Method for Training Actors." In *Acting (Re)Considered*, 2nd ed., edited by Phillip B. Zarrilli, 219–38. New York: Routledge, 2002.

Brady, James. "In Step with . . . Vincent D'Onofrio." *Parade*, April 11, 2004, 18.

Brestoff, Richard. *The Great Acting Teachers and Their Methods*. Lyme, N.H.: Smith and Kraus, 1995.

Brockett, Oscar G., and Robert Findlay. *Century of Innovation*. 2nd ed. Boston: Allyn and Bacon, 1991.

Carnicke, Sharon Marie. Interview by the authors. Tape recording. August 14, 2002.

———. *Stanislavsky in Focus*. Amsterdam: Harwood Academic Publishers, 1998.

Chamberlain, Franc. "Michael Chekhov on the Technique of Acting." In Hodge, *Twentieth Century Actor Training*, 83–86.

Chapman, Linda S. Interview by the authors. Tape recording. September 14, 2002.

Chekhov, Michael. *To the Actor: On the Technique of Acting*. New York: Harper & Row, 1953.

Chinoy, Helen Krich, and Virginia Scott, eds. "Reunion: A Self-Portrait of the Group Theatre." *Educational Theatre Journal* 28, no. 4 (December 1976).

Clurman, Harold. *The Fervent Years*. New York: Hill and Wang, 1957.

Coger, Leslie Irene. "Stanislavski Changes His Mind." In Munk, *Stanislavski and America*, 60–65.

Cole, Toby, comp. *Acting: A Handbook of the Stanislavski Method*. 2nd ed. New York: Crown, 1955. Originally published in 1947.

D'Onofrio, Elizabeth. Interview by the authors. Tape recording. August 14, 2002.

D'Onofrio, Vincent. Interview by the authors. Tape recording. January 17, 2005.

Edwards, Christine. *The Stanislavsky Heritage*. New York: New York University Press, 1965.

Gauss, Rebecca. *Lear's Daughters*. New York: Peter Lang, 1999.

Gorchakov, Nikolai M. *Stanislavsky Directs*. Translated by Miriam Goldina. New York: Funk & Wagnalls, 1954.

Gordon, Mel. *The Stanislavsky Technique*. New York: Applause Theatre Book Publishers, 1987.

Gray, Paul. "A Critical Anthology." In Munk, *Stanislavski and America*, 137–81.

———. "Stanislavski and America: A Critical Chronology." In "Stanislavski and America: 2," edited by Richard Schechner. Special issue, *TDR* 9, no. 2 (Winter 1964): 21–60.

Gussow, Mel. "Michael Chekhov's Life and Work." *TDR* 27, no. 3 (1983): 1–21.

Hagen, Uta. *A Challenge for the Actor*. New York: Scribner, 1991.

———. *Respect for Acting*. New York: Macmillan, 1973.

Harrop, John. "Stanislavski System and the 'Method.'" Review of *The Stanislavski System*, by Sonia Moore. *Theatre Quarterly* 7 (Spring 1977): 25.

Hodge, Allison, ed. *Twentieth Century Actor Training*. New York: Routledge, 2000.

Jilinsky, Andrius. *The Joy of Acting: A Primer for Actors*. Edited by Helen C. Bragdon. New York: Peter Lang, 1989.

Knebel, M. O. "Superior Simplicity." In Moore, *Stanislavski Today*, 44–47.

———. "The Nemirovitch-Dantchenko School of Directing." In Moore, *Stanislavski Today*, 48–55.

Kristi, Gregori V. "The Training of an Actor in the Stanislavski School of Acting." In Moore, *Stanislavski Today*, 22–33.

Kupferberg, Herbert. "The American Stanislavsky Theatre." Draft copy. Collection of Philip G. Bennett.

Law, Alma. "An Actor's Director Debuts in the West: A Conversation with Russia's Georgi Tovstonogov." *American Theatre* (June 1987): 17–19, 45.

Londré, Felicia. Interview by the authors. Tape recording. June 27, 2002.

———. "Sonia Moore." Unpublished manuscript. 1981. Private collection.

———. "Stanislavski's Champion: Sonia Moore and Her Crusade to Save the American Theatre." *Theatre History Studies* 24 (June 2004): 11–24.

Lund, Frone. Interview by the authors. Tape recording. July 25, 2002.

Marowitz, Charles. *The Other Chekhov: A Biography of Michael Chekhov, the Legendary Actor-Director and Theorist*. New York: Applause Theatre Books, 2004.

———. "The Michael Chekhov Twist." *American Theatre* (January 2005): 43–44, 122–23.

McTeague, James H. *Before Stanislavsky: American Professional Acting Schools and Theory, 1875–1924*. Metuchen, N.J.: Scarecrow Press, 1993.

Merlin, Bella. *Beyond Stanislavsky*. New York: Routledge / Theatre Arts Books, 2001.

———. *Konstantin Stanislavsky*. New York: Routledge, 2003.

Moore, Irene. Interview by the authors. Tape recording. March 20, 2002.

Moore, Sonia. "I Dared to Love, A Russian Memoir, 1917–1940." Unpublished manuscript. 1994, collection of Irene Moore.

———. "Konstantin Stanislavski." *The Stage and Television Today.* January 17, 1963, 14.

———. "The Method of Physical Actions." In Munk, *Stanislavski and America,* 73–76.

———. "A Reaction to T-57 Article on Stanislavsky." *TDR* 17, no. 2 (June 1973): 136.

———. *The Stanislavski Method.* New York: Viking Press, 1960.

———. *Stanislavski Revealed: The Actor's Guide to Spontaneity on Stage.* New York: Applause Theatre Book Publishers, 1991.

———. *The Stanislavski System.* New York: Viking Press, 1965. Rev. ed., New York: Penguin, 1974. 2nd rev. ed., 1984.

———, trans. and ed. *Stanislavski Today.* New York: American Center for Stanislavski Theatre Art, 1973.

———. *Training an Actor: The Stanislavski System in Class.* New York: Viking Press, 1968. Rev. ed. New York: Penguin Books, 1979.

Munk, Erica, ed. *Stanislavski and America.* New York: Hill and Wang, 1966.

———. "Stanislavski Preserved: An MAT Discussion." In Munk, *Stanislavski and America,* 66–73.

Playfare: ACSTA I. Vol. 3. New York: Playfare, March 1971.

Poggi, Jack. "The Stanislavsky System in Russia." *TDR* 17, no. 1 (March 1973): 124–33.

Roach, Joseph R. *The Player's Passion.* Newark: University of Delaware Press, 1985.

Robbins, Jane Marla. Interview by the authors. Tape recording. September 22, 2002.

Schechner, Richard. "Working with Live Material: An Interview with Lee Strasberg." In Moore, *Stanislavski and America,* 183–200.

Silver, Len. Interview by the authors. Tape recording. July 11, 2002.

Simonov, P. V. "The Method of K. S. Stanislavski and the Physiology of Emotion." In Munk, *Stanislavski Today,* 34–43.

———. "Methods of Physical Activities." *Interscaena* 2, no. 1 (1971): 21–43.

Soloviova, Inna. "Do You Have Relatives Living Abroad? Emigration as a Cultural Problem." In *Wandering Stars: Russian Emigré Theatre, 1905–1940,* edited by Laurence Senelick, 69–83. Iowa City: University of Iowa Press, 1992.

Sonia Moore Papers, New York Public Library for the Performing Arts.

The Sonia Moore Studio of the Theatre Student Handbook. New York: American Center for Stanislavski Theatre Art, n.d., collection of Elizabeth C. Stroppel.

Stanislavski, Constantin. *An Actor Prepares.* Translated by Elizabeth Reynolds Hapgood. New York: Theatre Arts Books, 1936.

———. *Building a Character.* Translated by Elizabeth Reynolds Hapgood. New York: Theatre Arts Books, 1949.

———. *Creating a Role.* Edited by Elizabeth Reynolds Hapgood. Translated by Hermione I. Popper. New York: Theatre Arts Books, 1961.

———. *Stanislavski's Legacy.* Edited and translated by Elizabeth Reynolds Hapgood. New York: Theatre Arts Books, 1958.

———. *Stanislavsky on the Art of the Stage.* Introduced and trans. by David Magarshack. 1950. New York: Hill and Wang, 1961.

"Tamara Daykarhanova School for the Stage." Tamara Daykarhanova Papers. New York Public Library for the Performing Arts.

Toporkov, Vasily. *Stanislavski in Rehearsal.* Translated by Christine Edwards. New York: Theatre Arts Books, 1979.

Wolf, Mary Hunter. "Reminiscences of Andrius Jilinsky and His Teaching." In Senelick, *Wandering Stars,* 129–39.

World Biographical Hall of Fame. Vol. 4. Rev. ed. Raleigh, N.C.: Historical Preservations of America, 1992.

Zarrilli, Phillip B., ed. *Acting (Re)Considered.* 2nd ed. New York: Routledge, 2002.

Index

About the Authors

Suzanne M. Trauth is a professor of theatre in the Department of Theatre and Dance, Montclair State University, Montclair, New Jersey, where she serves as coordinator of the BFA acting program, directing productions and teaching undergraduate and graduate courses in acting, dramatic literature, research methods, and screenwriting. She taught acting at the Sonia Moore Studio and directed plays in New York and in regional theatres. In addition to publishing articles on acting and directing theory and on Sonia Moore's work, she shared the platform with Sonia Moore at a variety of Association for Theatre in Higher Education conferences. She earned her MA and PhD degrees in theatre from Bowling Green State University.

Elizabeth C. Stroppel is an associate professor in the Department of Communication, of William Paterson University, Wayne, New Jersey, where she teaches classes in acting, playwriting, playscripts, and theatre history, serves as the director of theatre studies, directs, and dramaturgs. Her article "Reconciling the Past and the Present: Feminist Perspectives on the 'Method' in the Classroom and on the Stage," published in *Method Acting Revisited* (2000), highlights her dissertation research on acting from feminist perspectives. She received her PhD in theatre history and dramatic text and criticism from the University of Texas, Austin, and her MA in theatre from the University of South Carolina. Prior to that she taught acting at the Sonia Moore Studio and studied and performed professionally in New York City.